CULTIVATING THE SPIRIT

How College Can Enhance Students' Inner Lives

Alexander W. Astin

Helen S. Astin

Jennifer A. Lindholm

JOSSEY-BASS
A Wiley Imprint
www.josseybass.com

Published by Jossey-Bass
A Wiley Imprint
989 Market Street, San Francisco, CA 94103-1741—www.josseybass.com

Jossey-Bass books and products are available through most bookstores. To contact Jossey-Bass directly call our Customer Care Department within the U.S. at 800-956-7739, outside the U.S. at 317-572-3986, or fax 317-572-4002.

Jossey-Bass also publishes its books in a variety of electronic formats. Some content that appears in print may not be available in electronic books.

Portions of Chapter Two are taken from A. W. Astin, H. S. Astin, and J. A. Lindholm, "Assessing students' spiritual and religious qualities," *Journal of College Student Development*, in press. Reprinted with permission from the American College Personnel Association (ACPA), at the Center for Higher Education, One Dupont Circle, NW, Washington, DC 20036. Portions of Chapter Four are based on A. W. Astin and J. P. Keen, "Equanimity and spirituality," *Religion and Education*, *33*(2) (Spring 2006): 1–8.

Library of Congress Cataloging-in-Publication Data

Astin, Alexander W.
   Cultivating the spirit : how college can enhance students' inner lives / Alexander W. Astin, Helen S. Astin, Jennifer A. Lindholm.
       p. cm.
     Includes bibliographical references and index.
   ISBN 978-0-470-76933-1 (hardback)
   ISBN 978-0-470-87569-8 (ebk.)
   ISBN 978-0-470-87570-4 (ebk.)
   ISBN 978-0-470-87571-1 (ebk.)
   1. College students—Psychology.   2. College students—Religious life—United States.
3. Self-actualization (Psychology)—Religious aspects.   I. Astin, Helen S., 1932-   II. Lindholm, Jennifer A., 1968-   III. Title.
   LB3609.A78 2010
   378.1'98019—dc22

                                                                          2010028491

Printed in the United States of America
FIRST EDITION
HB Printing   10 9 8 7 6 5 4 3

CONTENTS

To our granddaughters, Erin, Amalia, and Ila
—Alexander Astin and Helen Astin

To Mom, Cooper, and Bentley
—Jennifer Lindholm

ABOUT THE AUTHORS

Psychologist Alexander W. Astin is the Allan M. Cartter Distinguished Professor of Higher Education, Emeritus, at the University of California at Los Angeles (UCLA). He is also the founding director of the Higher Education Research Institute at UCLA and the author of twenty-one books and more than four hundred other publications. His research and writing in the field of higher education has earned him awards from thirteen different national associations.

Readers of *Change* magazine voted Dr. Astin as the person "most admired for creative, insightful thinking" in the field of higher education. A study in the *Journal of Higher Education* identified him as the most frequently cited author in the higher education field, and his book *Four Critical Years* as the most frequently cited book in the field. Astin has lectured at more than 250 colleges and universities in the United States and abroad, served as a fellow at the Center for Advanced Study in the Behavioral Sciences at Stanford University, been elected to membership in the National Academy of Education, and is the recipient of eleven honorary degrees.

Helen S. Astin, a psychologist, is Distinguished Professor Emerita of Higher Education and Senior Scholar in the Higher Education Research Institute at UCLA. She has served as the associate provost of the College of Letters and Science at UCLA and as director of the UCLA Center for the Study of Women. Dr. Astin is a trustee of Mount St. Mary's College and has served as a trustee of Hampshire College. In the American Psychological Association she has been president of the Division of the Psychology of Women.

Astin is a recipient of the Distinguished Research Award of Division J of the American Educational Research Association and the Howard Bowen Distinguished Career Award from the Association for the Study of Higher Education. Her research and writings have focused on issues of equity and inclusion with a special emphasis on gender inequities, leadership, the faculty reward structure, and spirituality. Among her books are *Women of Influence, Women of Vision; Human Resources and Higher Education; The Woman Doctorate in America; Higher Education and the Disadvantaged Student;* and *Some Action on Her Own: The Adult Woman and Higher Education.*

Jennifer A. Lindholm is special assistant to the Vice Provost for Undergraduate Education at UCLA and director of the Spirituality in Higher Education project. From 2001 to 2006 she served as associate director of the Cooperative Institutional Research Program at UCLA's Higher Education Research Institute and as director of the institute's Triennial National Faculty Survey. Dr. Lindholm also served as visiting professor of higher education and organizational change in UCLA's Graduate School of Education & Information Studies.

Lindholm's publications focus on the structural and cultural dimensions of academic work; the career development, work experiences, and professional behavior of college and university faculty; issues related to institutional change; and undergraduate students' personal development.

ACKNOWLEDGMENTS

This book is based on a seven-year study very generously supported by the John Templeton Foundation. We are especially grateful to Arthur Schwartz, formerly executive vice president at the foundation, who approached us eight years ago with the idea of undertaking this national study of students' search for meaning and purpose. Thank you, Arthur, for your enormous support and early guidance in conceptualizing the study and for challenging us to think critically, creatively, and expansively. Kimon Sargeant, vice president of human sciences, has served as the foundation's project officer over the past four years. We appreciate his trust in us and his willingness to be a supportive facilitator of this work. We also appreciate the interest and support of Pamela Thompson, vice president of communications.

From the start, we were fortunate to have two groups of advisors: a Technical Advisory Panel (TAP) of scholars in the field of religion and spirituality and a National Advisory Board (NAB) that included national leaders from the field of higher education. From the TAP we owe a special debt of gratitude to John Astin, Arthur Chickering, Peter Hill, Ellen Idler, Cynthia Johnson, Mike McCullough, Scotty McLennan, Ken Pargament, and Christian Smith for their help and wise counsel through all stages of the project. Members of our NAB, including Rebecca Chopp, James Fowler, Claire Gaudiani, Nathan Hatch, Arthur Levine, Carol Geary Schneider, David Scott, Huston Smith, Beverly Tatum, Diana Chapman Walsh, and William Willimon, not only served as sounding boards but also provided helpful advice at crucial stages of the work.

We also want to thank Ken Wilber for several helpful suggestions concerning the design of our pilot survey instrument. David Brightman, senior editor at Jossey-Bass, was very helpful in expediting the review and production of our manuscript. Our copy editor, Jeffrey Wyneken, also made a number of very helpful suggestions. Throughout the study we have worked closely with colleagues at Widmeyer Communications, who helped in many ways to communicate our findings to the larger public and to make our project more visible nationally.

During all phases of the project we have also been very fortunate to have worked with a number of very talented graduate students from UCLA's Higher Educational and Organizational Change program: Alyssa Bryant, Shannon Calderone, Christopher Collins, Estella Gutierrez-Zamano, Jennifer Mallen, Kyle McJunkin, Lisa Millora, Nida Denson, Julie Park, Leslie Schwartz, Hanna Song Spinosa, and Katalin Szelényi. Their help in virtually all phases of this project has been critical, and they will all remain our friends and colleagues. Our heartfelt thanks to all of you and our warmest best wishes as you continue your careers as teachers, scholars, and higher education professionals.

The administration and staff of the Higher Education Research Institute and the Graduate School of Education & Information Studies have also been an important part of the success of this study. Special thanks to Kit Mahoney, Carmen Kistner, Mary Rabb, Thomas Rimbach, and Anna Pearl for their loyalty and critical assistance with the many administrative aspects of this project. Kathy Wyer was also very helpful in providing us with critical editorial assistance in the preparation of this book. Thank you, Kathy, for your sharp eye, wise suggestions, enthusiasm, and overall support.

Finally, we want to express our deepest gratitude to all the institutions and especially to the students and faculty who participated in the study. Without your thoughtful responses to our surveys and interviews, this study would not have been possible.

CULTIVATING THE SPIRIT

CHAPTER ONE

WHY SPIRITUALITY MATTERS

This book is about the spiritual growth of college students. It is based on a seven-year study of how students change during the college years and the role that college plays in facilitating the development of their spiritual qualities.

Our primary reason for undertaking this study has been our shared belief that *spirituality is fundamental to students' lives.* The "big questions" that preoccupy students are essentially spiritual questions: Who am I? What are my most deeply felt values? Do I have a mission or purpose in my life? Why am I in college? What kind of person do I want to become? What sort of world do I want to help create? When we speak of students' "spiritual quest," we are essentially speaking of their efforts to seek answers to such questions.

How students deal with these questions has obvious implications for many very practical decisions that they will have to make, including their choices of courses, majors, and careers, not to mention whether they opt to stay in college or drop out and whether they decide to pursue postgraduate study. Seeking answers to these questions is also directly relevant to the development of personal qualities such as self-understanding, empathy, caring, and social responsibility.

Despite the extraordinary amount of research that has been done on the development of college students (Pascarella and Terenzini, 1991, 2005)—more than five thousand studies in the past four decades—very little systematic study has been done on students' spiritual development. Indeed, in the latest comprehensive review of the literature that examines the effect of college on students (Pascarella and Terenzini, 2005), there are no references to "spirituality" and only two references to "religion." Recent years have seen a surge of interest in the topic of spirituality among some scholars and practitioners in higher education (Braskamp, Trautvetter, and Ward, 2006; Chickering, Dalton, and Stamm, 2005; Kazanjian and Laurence, 2000; Tisdell, 2003), but aside from a few studies of students' religious development conducted mainly at religiously affiliated colleges, very little empirical research has been done on students' spiritual development. We were thus motivated to undertake this study in part because of this gap in the literature and our desire to shed some light on a little-understood but potentially very important topic.

This lack of interest in spirituality within the research community is likewise evident in our colleges and universities. While higher education continues to put a lot of emphasis on test scores, grades, credits, and degrees, it has increasingly come to neglect its students' "inner" development—the sphere of values and beliefs, emotional maturity, moral development, spirituality, and of self-understanding. For us, *how* students define their spirituality or *what* particular meaning they make of their lives is not at issue. Rather, our concern is that the relative amount of attention that colleges and universities devote to the "inner" and "outer" aspects of our students' lives has gotten way out of balance.

What is most ironic about all of this is that while many of the great literary and philosophical traditions that constitute the core of a liberal education are grounded in the maxim, "know thyself," the development of self-awareness receives very little attention in our colleges and universities. If students lack self-understanding—the capacity to see themselves clearly and honestly and to understand why they feel and act as they do—then how can we expect them to become responsible parents, professionals, and citizens?

Another consideration that stimulated our interest in studying students' spiritual development is the manner in which students' concerns and values have been changing over recent decades. Annual surveys of entering college freshmen (Pryor et al., 2007) show that the personal goal of "being very well off financially" has grown dramatically in popularity, while the value of "developing a meaningful philosophy of life"—which was the highest-ranked concern in the 1970s—has declined sharply among students. This is not completely surprising to us. Over time, students have become more anxious about their futures and more overwhelmed by everything they have to do, balancing school with paid employment, worrying about being able to finance their college education and finding a job after college. At the same time, these personal concerns are exacerbated by national and global changes: a deteriorating economy, an environment that is being depleted of its natural resources, and religious and political conflicts that result in bloodshed and destruction around the globe.

Despite what seems to be a growing materialism and declining concern with existential questions among our college students, the study reported in this book shows that most students still maintain a strong interest in spiritual and religious matters. Fully four in five students tell us that they "have an interest in spirituality" and that they "believe in the sacredness of life," and nearly two-thirds say that "my spirituality is a source of joy." Students also hold strong religious beliefs. More than three-fourths believe in God, and more than two in three say that their religious/spiritual beliefs "provide me with strength, support, and guidance." Finally, three-fourths of the students report feeling a "sense of connection with God/Higher Power that transcends my personal self."

When they enter college as new freshmen, students also express high expectations for their own spiritual development. More than eight in ten report that "to find my purpose in life" is at least a "somewhat" important reason for attending college (half say it's a "very important" reason), and two-thirds of new freshmen say that it is either "very important" or "essential" that college "helps you develop your personal values" and "enhances your self-understanding."

Despite their strong religious orientation, today's students demonstrate a high level of religious tolerance and acceptance. Nine in ten college juniors agree that "non-religious people can lead lives that are just as moral as those of religious believers," and three in four agree that "most people can grow spiritually without being religious." Our study reveals that most students are searching for deeper meaning in their lives, looking for ways to cultivate their inner selves, seeking to be compassionate and charitable, and clarifying how they feel about the many issues confronting their society and the global community.

WHAT DO WE MEAN BY "SPIRITUALITY"?

Spirituality points to our inner, subjective life, as contrasted with the objective domain of observable behavior and material objects that we can point to and measure directly. Spirituality also involves our affective experiences at least as much as it does our reasoning or logic. More specifically, spirituality has to do with the values that we hold most dear, our sense of who we are and where we come from, our beliefs about why we are here—the meaning and purpose that we see in our work and our life—and our sense of connectedness to one another and to the world around us. Spirituality can also bear on aspects of our experience that are not easy to define or talk about, such things as intuition, inspiration, the mysterious, and the mystical. Finally, we believe that highly "spiritual" people tend to exemplify certain personal qualities such as love, compassion, and equanimity.

Since a casual perusal of a few dictionaries or a brief journey through the Internet, as well as a thorough review of the published scholarly literature, makes it clear that "spirituality" is subject to a variety of definitions, we make no claim that our definition is the only or even the ideal one. However, we do believe that it captures many of the basic elements that others have identified as components of spirituality. (A review of the literature shows that researchers and practitioners have defined spirituality as a dynamic construct that involves the internal process of seeking personal authenticity, genuineness, and wholeness; transcending one's locus of centricity while developing a greater sense of connectedness to self and others through relationship and community; deriving meaning, purpose, and direction in life; being open to exploring a relationship with a higher power that transcends human existence and human knowing; and valuing the sacred. Spirituality has also been described as an animating, creative, energizing, and meaning-making force; a source of inner strength; an inner moral orientation; a way of knowing and of being in the world; a source of connection that brings faith, hope, peace, and empowerment; and a dynamic expression of ourselves that gives shape to, and is shaped by, who we really are. Within the spiritual domain, human development has been characterized both by one's capacity to integrate the many other—cognitive, social, emotional, moral—aspects of development as well as our capacity for integrity, wholeness, openness, self-responsibility, and authentic self-transcendence. See, for example, Dyson, Cobb, and Forman, 1997; Goddard, 2000; Hill et al., 2000; Hindman, 2002; King, 1996; Baker, 2003; Love and Talbot, 1999; Tanyi, 2002; Zinnbauer, Pargament, and Scott, 1999; Parks, 2000; Zohar and Marshall, 2004.) We offer our brief characterization of spirituality here so that readers will have some sense of the perspective from which we have approached our study.

For many years, the construct of spirituality was closely aligned—even synonymous—with religious beliefs and convictions. Current conceptions, however, are much broader. How then do spirituality and religion differ? We see religiousness as involving adherence to a set of faith-based beliefs (and related practices) concerning both the origins of the world and the nature of the entity or being that is believed to have created and govern the world. Religiousness typically involves membership in some kind of community of fellow believers and practitioners, as well as participation in ceremonies or rituals This vision parallels distinctions made by other scholars, including those who compose the Institute/National Institute on Aging Workgroup: "Whereas religion is characterized by group activity that involves specific behavioral, social, doctrinal, and denominational characteristics, spirituality is commonly conceived as personal, transcendent, and characterized by qualities of relatedness" (Fetzer Institute, 2003). It is to be expected that some students will view religious practice as the primary means for expressing their spirituality, while for others formal religion will play little or no part in their spiritual life (see, for example, Fuller, 2001).

SPIRITUALITY AND HIGHER EDUCATION

When we speak of spirituality with our academic colleagues, we get highly varied responses. Some are uncomfortable with the term. Others are pleased that we are studying this aspect of students' lives. Still others tell us that spiritual issues have no place in the academy. Part of the problem is that the word "spirituality" is not likely to be heard in academic conversations; it's something new, and many academics are inclined to question something that is new or unfamiliar. There is also a deeper reason why academics are not likely to discuss spirituality: many faculty members associate spirituality with religion, and since most of our colleges and universities are secular, they assume that spirituality (religion) has no place in the academic environment, except possibly as a subject to be taught or studied by people in departments of religious studies. Academics who hold this view sometimes argue that a secular institution should not concern itself with its students' spirituality (religiousness) because "this is none of our business." Of course, such an extreme position ignores the fact that colleges and universities are already deeply involved with students' personal lives through such varied activities as academic advising, orientation, residential living, multicultural workshops, and "freshman 101" courses. Such activities necessarily touch on students' purposes, hopes, dreams, aspirations, values, beliefs, and other "spiritual" matters. Furthermore, the mission statements of colleges and universities frequently include a commitment to value-laden student outcomes like character, social responsibility, honesty, and citizenship.

In many respects, the secular institution is the ideal place for students to explore their spiritual sides because, unlike many sectarian institutions, there is no official perspective or dogma when it comes to spiritual values or beliefs. Students are presumably free, if not encouraged, to explore and question their values and beliefs, no matter where such questioning might lead them. Critics of secular institutions sometimes argue, of course, that such institutions do in fact promote a kind of de facto "party line"—a positivistic, materialistic, agnostic/atheistic perspective that discourages many students from openly exploring spiritual matters. While no doubt there are individual professors who embrace such views (and some who make little or no effort to hide them from students), many others do not share them. In fact, the national faculty survey that we conducted for this project shows that 81 percent of teaching faculty consider themselves to be "spiritual," and 64 percent, "religious" (Lindholm, Astin, and Astin, 2005).

To ignore the spiritual side of students' and faculty's lives is to encourage a kind of fragmentation and a lack of authenticity, where students and faculty act either as if they are not spiritual beings, or as if their spiritual side is irrelevant to their vocation or work. Within such an environment, academic endeavors can become separated from students' most deeply felt values, and students may hesitate to discuss issues of meaning, purpose, authenticity, and wholeness with each other and especially with faculty.

This kind of fragmentation is further encouraged by those who believe that higher education should concern itself only with students' "cognitive" development—thinking, reasoning, memorizing, critical analysis, and the like—and that the affective or emotional side of the student's life is not relevant to the work of the university. We do not believe that there is any such thing as "pure" cognition that can be considered in isolation from affect; on the contrary, it would appear that our thoughts and our reasoning are almost always taking place in some kind of affective "bed" or context.

In the past few years, higher education has come under increasing criticism for what many see as its impersonal and fragmented approach to undergraduate education. Growing numbers of educators are calling for a more holistic education, pointing to the need to connect mind and spirit and to return to the true values of liberal education—an education that examines learning and knowledge in relation to an exploration of self (see, for example, Braskamp, Trautvetter, and Ward, 2006; Chickering, Dalton, and Stamm, 2005; Lee, 1999; Tisdell, 2003; Trautvetter, 2007). Such a reinvigorated liberal arts curriculum would, of course, pay much closer attention to the existential questions that we know are prominent in students' minds. At the same time, we have seen a movement gradually emerging in higher education where many academics find themselves actively searching for meaning and trying to discover ways to make their lives and their institutions more whole. This movement likely reflects a growing concern with recovering a sense of meaning in American society more generally. The growing unease about our institutions and our society has led some of us to start talking much more openly about spirituality.

Envisioning campus communities in which the life of the mind and the life of the spirit are mutually celebrated, supported, and sustained necessitates that those of us within higher education reconsider our traditional ways of being and doing. We must be open to broadening our existing frames of reference and willing to look closely not just at what we do (or do not do) on a daily basis, but why. At the same time, persons outside the academy must also reflect on the origins of their traditional presumptions about the nature and purpose of higher education as well as their own academic experience and how it has affected their lives.

SPIRITUALITY AND THE GLOBAL SOCIETY

Since higher education is responsible for educating the next generation of leaders, it is reasonable to ask: What kinds of people will our global society need? It goes without saying that technical knowledge and technical skills are becoming increasingly important for one's effective functioning in modern society, but technical knowledge alone will not be adequate for dealing with some of society's most pressing problems: violence, poverty, crime, divorce, substance abuse, and the religious, national, and ethnic conflicts that continue to plague our country and our world. At root, these are problems of the spirit, problems that call for greater self-awareness, self-understanding, equanimity, empathy, and concern for others. A key aim of our study is to assess how and why these qualities change during the college years and the role college plays in their development. The findings from the study reported in this book should not only teach us more about what colleges and universities can do to promote students' spiritual growth but also enhance our understanding of how spiritual development can contribute to global understanding and caring.

The book is written with a diverse audience in mind. While the higher education community may well turn out to be our primary audience, we also believe that parents and students themselves could also regard the findings to be of considerable interest. Indeed, our view is that the larger public would also benefit from learning about students' ongoing search for meaning and purpose, about their need to care for and about others, their interest in and appreciation of the global community and the environment, and their quest for feeling more whole, more centered, and more at peace with themselves and others.

THE STUDY

The main objectives of the study reported in this book are to document how students change spiritually and religiously during the college years, and to identify ways in which colleges can contribute to this developmental process. Our hope is that the knowledge generated by this research will enhance higher education's capacity to facilitate students' spiritual development.

We began this work in 2003. At the outset, we wanted the research to be comprehensive, to cover students of different racial and religious backgrounds and in different fields of study. We also wanted our students' colleges to reflect the wonderful diversity of America's higher education institutions—public and private, large and small, selective and nonselective, religious and nonreligious. To study such a large and diverse sample of students, we obviously had to utilize a survey approach, whereby students would tell us about themselves and their college experiences via self-administered survey questionnaires. Our first task was to develop a survey questionnaire that could explore the student's spiritual life and religious beliefs and practices. This process, which is described in detail in Chapter Two, initially involved a great deal of reading, discussion, pilot testing, and consultation with colleagues across the country.

Data from a pilot survey conducted in 2003 with about 3,700 college students were used to develop measures of students' spiritual and religious qualities. Next we surveyed over 112,000 students in Fall 2004. Finally, a subsample of about 15,000 of these students completed another survey as they were about to finish their junior year in Spring 2007. The main purpose of the 2004 and 2007 surveys was to create a longitudinal database, which would enable us to assess changes in individual students' spiritual and religious qualities during the first three years of college. To supplement the rich data that these students provided in the two surveys, we also conducted personal interviews and focus groups with students enrolled in eleven diverse campuses across the country. Selected faculty from each campus were also interviewed.

In an effort to understand the role that college faculty play in affecting students' spiritual development, during the 2004–2005 academic year we also collected extensive survey data from individual faculty members at the same institutions where we collected longitudinal student data. This survey examined each faculty member's spirituality, goals for undergraduate education, preferred teaching styles, and attitudes about the potential role that institutions might play in facilitating the student's spiritual development.

THE STORY

We believe that the story told by our study data is not only fascinating but also of great importance for students, for institutions, and for the larger society. Essentially, we find that while students' degree of religious engagement declines somewhat during college, their spirituality shows substantial growth. Students become more caring, more tolerant, more connected with others, and more actively engaged in a spiritual quest. We have also found that *spiritual growth enhances other college outcomes*, such as academic performance, psychological well-being, leadership development, and satisfaction with college.

These positive changes in students' spiritual qualities are not merely maturational; indeed, our data provide strong evidence pointing to specific experiences during college that can contribute to students' spiritual growth. Some of these experiences, such as study abroad, interdisciplinary studies, and service learning, appear to be effective because they expose students to new and diverse people, cultures, and ideas. Spiritual development is also enhanced if students engage in what we refer to as "inner work" through activities such as meditation or self-reflection, or if their professors actively encourage them to explore questions of meaning and purpose. In contrast, our data suggest that spiritual development is impeded when students engage in activities that distract them from the ordinary experience of campus life—activities such as watching a lot of television or spending a good deal of time playing video games.

OUTLINE OF THE BOOK

In the next chapter, we describe how we developed ten different measures of students' spiritual and religious qualities. The next five chapters (Three–Seven) document how students change spiritually and religiously during the first three years of college, and how specific aspects of the college experience help to shape their spiritual and religious development. Chapter Eight examines the role of spiritual development in students' academic and personal development, and Chapter Nine discusses what institutions can and are doing to assist students in their spiritual journey.

CHAPTER TWO

ASSESSING SPIRITUAL AND RELIGIOUS QUALITIES

Surveys ordinarily consist of a number of short questions that don't require long answers, such as, "Do you believe in God?" to which someone might respond by checking a box: yes, no, or not sure. A survey approach to studying people is useful in that a lot of questions can be asked in a relatively short time. It is essential, however, to ask the right set of questions—questions that cover the territory well—and to ask them in a way that makes sense to the people you're studying, so that you may draw meaningful conclusions from their answers. When using a survey questionnaire to explore something as complex and personal as a student's spirituality or religiousness, not only is it necessary to ask a lot of questions, but the questions must also be phrased so that they make sense to Christians, Muslims, Hindus, agnostics, and atheists alike. And once the answers have been compiled, it's critical that taken together they bear some significance, so that valid conclusions may be drawn about each student's spiritual and religious life.

Let's illustrate how we approached this task by looking at religiousness. Our survey questionnaire necessarily included a question about the student's religious affiliation (Baptist, Buddhist, Jewish, Roman Catholic, none, and so on), but that was not enough; it was also necessary to determine the degree of religiousness, or how religious a given student was. Many questions must be asked in order to get a comprehensive picture of a student's religious life, and since students can express their religious inclinations in many ways, some questions should focus on the strength of their religious faith, such as whether they seek to follow religious teachings in their everyday life, or how connected they feel to a higher power; and some questions should inquire about their behavior, including how much they pray, or how often they participate in religious rituals or services. We ultimately asked students approximately sixty short questions that directly related to their religiousness. And because of the emphasis given by many religious leaders to certain controversial, hot-button issues, we also asked a dozen or so additional questions that addressed casual sex, abortion, and homosexuality.

How then do we draw meaningful conclusions about how religious each student is from his or her answers to these sixty or seventy-five questions? We could, of course, simply make a long list of the student's answers to each question, but that would constitute an almost incomprehensible mass of data. A better approach is to combine the student's answers into a scale that reflects that student's degree of religiousness. Thus, students who report that they "frequently" attend religious services, pray "frequently," "frequently" read sacred texts, and so on would receive a high score on the Religiousness scale, while students who report that they "never" do such things would receive a low score. Students who report that they "sometimes" engage in such activities would receive a middle-range score. Statistical analyses[1] enabled us to use twenty-eight of the questions about religion to construct three scales that reflect different ways in which students express their degree of religiousness: Religious Commitment, Religious Engagement, and Religious/Social Conservatism. Chapter Six covers these measures in detail. We also found that we could use some of the remaining questions about religion to construct two additional scales, which we called Religious Skepticism and Religious Struggle; these are discussed in Chapter Seven.

Since spirituality is a more complex and abstract concept than religiousness, we devised even more questions having to do with spirituality, such as, "Are you currently searching for meaning and purpose in life?" with possible answers being: to a great extent; to some extent; or not at all. In developing items that addressed students' spiritual qualities, we were guided by two basic principles: one, that spirituality is a multidimensional construct and that no single measure can adequately capture all that we mean when we use the term (see, for example, Elkins et al., 1988; Hill et al., 2000; MacDonald, 2000); and two, that while many students no doubt express their spirituality in terms of some form of organized religion, the fact that others do not requires that we view religiousness and spirituality as separate qualities, and that we attempt to develop separate measures of each.

In short, the fundamental task we set for ourselves was to design a survey questionnaire that could provide us with a comprehensive look at each student's spiritual and religious qualities. The original research team for the project, which included the authors together with an advanced doctoral student, Kati Szelényi, worked closely with our Technical Advisory Panel[2] to design the survey. Our approach to this task might be characterized as one of "informed consensus." That is, by informing ourselves about the considerable literature in this field, by consulting regularly with expert researchers in this field (our Technical Advisory Panel), and by engaging in an ongoing dialogue to share with each other what we were learning, we could best assure that we would develop a set of survey items that adequately reflected students' spiritual and religious qualities. Accordingly, in the year leading up to the development of the pilot survey, our research team read a good deal of literature on spirituality, participated in a UCLA graduate seminar on spirituality in higher education, and took part in a number of brainstorming sessions concerning the meaning and measurement of spirituality.

The process of survey development began with an exploration of various definitions of "spirituality" proposed by scholars in business, education, health, psychology, sociology, and other fields (see, for example, Ashmos and Duchon, 2000; Baker, 2003; Burack, 1999; Cannister, 1998; Cook et al., 2000; Dehler and Welsh, 1997; Dyson, Cobb, and Forman, 1997; Gibbons, 2000; Hayes, 1984; Hill and Pargament, 2003; Hodge, 2003; Krahnke and Hoffman, 2002; Love and Talbot, 1999; Maher and Hunt, 1993; Pargament, 1999; Rose, 2001). Because a number of psychologists and measurement specialists have also attempted to develop measures of "spirituality" and "religiousness" during the past decade, this critical body of work was reviewed as well. One key resource on which the research team relied heavily in developing the new survey was Hill and Hood's comprehensive analysis of 125 different scales that have been developed in this area of research (Hill and Hood, 1999). Our team examined every item in every scale. Although our evaluation of these instruments indicated that they contained a number of interesting and potentially useful items, no single instrument appeared to be well suited to the purposes of this project.

The limitations inherent in many of these instruments were expressed in different ways. For example, "spirituality" is often equated with traditional religious practice and beliefs. Questions often assume, either explicitly or implicitly, that the respondent embraces a monotheistic, Judeo-Christian belief system (Moberg, 2002). Additionally, no distinction is made between one's spirituality and one's theological perspective, nor is a distinction made between "inner" and "outer" manifestations of spirituality, that is, between spiritual attitudes, beliefs, or perspectives, and spiritual action or behavior.

In developing the new survey instrument, the research team sought to design a set of questions that would meet the following requirements:

- No assumptions would be made about the student's religious/spiritual perspective, or lack thereof. All students—regardless of their theological/metaphysical perspective or belief system—should be able to respond to items in a meaningful way.
- References to "God," "supreme being," or a similar entity would be held to a minimum; rather, students would be given an opportunity to specify what such a concept means to them, including an option to reject the concept.
- Both religious beliefs/perspectives and religious practices/behaviors would be covered, although the use of specific denominational or sectarian terminology would be avoided (for example, "sacred texts" would be used instead of "Bible" or "Koran").
- The items would accommodate those who define their spirituality primarily in terms of conventional religious beliefs and practices as well as those who define their spirituality in other ways.

TWELVE CONTENT AREAS, OR DOMAINS

Preliminary work resulted in the identification of twelve content areas or "domains" to be considered in designing items and scales to measure spirituality and religiousness. The examples provided here illustrate how an item that relates to a specific domain might appear on the survey questionnaire:

- Spiritual or religious outlook (orientation/worldview)

  Example: "Love is at the root of all the great religions"

- Spiritual well-being

  Example: "I see each day, good or bad, as a gift"

- Spiritual/religious behavior/practice

  Example: "I pray on a daily basis"

- Self-assessments

  Example: "Rate yourself, in comparison to others your age, on each of the following traits: religiousness, spirituality, etc."

- Compassionate behavior

  Example: "How frequently do you participate in community service work?"

- Sense of connectedness to others and the world

  Example: "I feel a strong connection to all humanity"

- Spiritual quest

  Example: "How frequently do you have discussions about the meaning of life with friends?"

- Spiritual/mystical experiences

  Example: "Have you ever had a 'spiritual' experience while listening to beautiful music?"

- Facilitators/inhibitors of spiritual development

Example: "Since entering college, which of the following experiences have changed your religious/spiritual beliefs: interactions with faculty, course content, etc."

- Theological/metaphysical beliefs

Example: "Do you believe in life after death?"

- Attitudes toward religion/spirituality

Example: "Most people can grow spiritually without being religious"

- Religious affiliation/identity

Example: "Identify your religious identity: Baptist, Buddhist, Catholic, etc." (twenty choices, including "none" and "other")

Using these domains as a framework, we developed a large number of potential survey items. In addition to modifying many of the items developed by earlier investigators, we also created a number of new items. Throughout this process, Technical Advisory Panel members and the research team served as "judges" in finalizing the relevant domains and selecting the most appropriate items for each domain. All of this preliminary work led to the development of a pilot survey that included approximately 175 items having to do with spirituality and religion and 50–60 other items covering students' activities and achievements since entering college as well as posttests on selected items from the freshman survey questionnaire these same students had completed three years earlier (in Fall 2000) when they entered college.

The resulting four-page questionnaire, which we called the College Students' Beliefs and Values (CSBV) Survey, was completed by 3,680 college juniors attending a diverse sample of forty-six baccalaureate colleges and universities in Spring 2003; this institutional sample was designed to ensure diversity with respect to type (colleges and universities), control (public, private-nonsectarian, Roman Catholic, Protestant, Evangelical), and selectivity level. Survey administration details are provided in the Appendix.

Developing Measures of Spirituality and Religiousness

Once students had completed and returned their 2003 CSBV surveys and the resulting data were prepared for analysis, our next major task was to develop "scales" by searching for clusters of survey items that formed coherent patterns in how students responded. To illustrate what we mean by a pattern, let's consider Religious Struggle. This measure, or scale, consists of seven items that are positively correlated with one another, meaning that there is a consistent pattern in how students respond. By "consistent" we mean that if a given student endorses one item from the scale, such as, "I feel unsettled about spiritual and religious matters," that student will tend to endorse other items in the scale as well: "I've questioned my religious/spiritual beliefs," "I felt distant from God," "I disagreed with my family about religious matters," and so on. Such a student would obtain a high score on Religious Struggle. In contrast, if a student did not endorse these and other items in the scale, that student would obtain a low score on Religious Struggle.

Our principal means of identifying such patterns was a statistical method known as factor analysis,[3] a procedure that examines the correlations among a set of variables (in this case, individual questionnaire items) with the aim of reducing the variables to a smaller set of more general "factors," or scales. Compared to individual items, scales have at least two other advantages. Primarily, they are more reliable measures of religiousness and spirituality than individual items, but they also facilitate the task of interpreting results. Because there is likely to be a good deal of redundancy in the students' responses to 175 items, it becomes much easier to make sense out of the results if these items can be reduced to a much smaller number of multi-item scales (Moberg, 2002). Our analyses identified more than a dozen clusters of items, but for purposes here we focus on ten—five measures of spiritual development and five measures of religious development—each of which is addressed in the chapters of this book.

The five spiritual measures include Spiritual Quest, Equanimity, Ethic of Caring, Charitable Involvement, and Ecumenical

Worldview. The five measures of religious qualities are Religious Commitment, Religious Engagement, Religious/Social Conservatism, Religious Skepticism, and Religious Struggle. For a complete list of all the items that constitute each measure, see the Appendix.

THE LONGITUDINAL STUDY

Once we had identified our ten measures using data from the pilot (2003 CSBV) survey, we undertook a much larger-scale survey involving freshmen entering 236 baccalaureate-granting institutions in the fall of 2004. This revised CSBV Survey, which was a slightly modified version of the pilot survey, was completed by 112,232 entering first-year students as a two-page addendum to the four-page freshman survey administered annually by the Cooperative Institutional Research Program (CIRP) at UCLA's Higher Education Research Institute (Sax et al., 2004). Data from this normative sample were ultimately weighted to approximate the responses we would have expected had all first-time, full-time students attending baccalaureate colleges and universities across the country participated in the survey.

The third and final administration of the CSBV involved a longitudinal follow-up of students from 136 of the 236 institutions that had participated in the 2004 freshman survey. These institutions were chosen so that we had roughly equal numbers of institutions by selectivity level, type (colleges and universities), and control (public, private nonsectarian, Roman Catholic, Evangelical, and other religious—primarily "mainline" Protestant). Samples of students who had completed the 2004 freshman survey were randomly selected from each institution for this longitudinal follow-up. These students were surveyed in the late spring of 2007, at the end of their third year. Completed surveys were eventually received from a total of 14,527 students at 136 institutions, representing an overall 40 percent response rate among those who were asked to complete the follow-up survey. A complex weighting system was applied to the follow-up data to approximate the results that would have been obtained if all 2007 "juniors" (2004 entering freshmen who were still enrolled in 2007) at baccalaureate-granting institutions in the United States had responded to the follow-up. All findings reported in this book are based on weighted results. For complete administrative and methodological details pertaining to both the 2004 freshman survey and the 2007 longitudinal follow-up survey, see the Appendix.

When we analyzed the 14,527 students' responses to the 2004 freshman survey and the 2007 follow-up survey, we found that we could readily reproduce the same ten measures that we developed in the 2003 pilot survey; the students' responses to the individual items in both of the later surveys formed patterns that were almost identical to the patterns identified in the pilot survey. This gave us confidence that we were dealing with measures that carried wide application.

MEASURES OF SPIRITUALITY

A first group of spirituality measures focuses on two "internally" directed aspects of students' spirituality:

Spiritual Quest is a nine-item measure that assesses the student's interest in searching for meaning/purpose in life, finding answers to the mysteries of life, attaining inner harmony, and developing a meaningful philosophy of life. The notion of a spiritual quest is clearly reflected in the prevalence of words such as "finding," "attaining," "seeking," "developing," "searching," and "becoming."

Equanimity includes five items reflecting the extent to which the student feels at peace or is centered, is able to find meaning in times of hardship, sees each day as a gift, and feels good about the direction of her/his life. Elsewhere we have argued that equanimity may well be the prototypic defining quality of a spiritual person (Astin and Keen, 2006).

The second set of spirituality measures are "externally" directed aspects, focusing on students' connectedness to those around them, and reflecting "caring about" and "caring for" one another:

Ethic of Caring is an eight-item measure that assesses the student's degree of commitment to values such as helping others in difficulty, reducing pain and suffering in the world, promoting racial understanding, trying to change things that are unfair in the world, and making the world a better place.

Charitable Involvement is a seven-item behavioral measure that includes activities such as participating in community service, donating money to charity, and helping friends with personal problems.

Ecumenical Worldview is a twelve-item measure that indicates the extent to which the student is interested in different religious traditions, seeks to understand other countries and cultures, feels a strong connection to all humanity, believes in the goodness of all people, accepts others as they are, and believes that all life is interconnected and that love is at the root of all the great religions.

MEASURES OF RELIGIOUSNESS

Religious Commitment is an internal quality comprising twelve items. It reflects the student's self-rating on "religiousness" as well as the degree to which the student seeks to follow religious teachings in everyday life, finds religion to be personally helpful, and gains personal strength by trusting in a higher power. In particular, it measures the extent to which "my spiritual/religious beliefs" play a central role in the student's life.

Religious Engagement, an external measure that represents the behavioral counterpart to Religious Commitment, includes nine items reflecting behaviors such as attending religious services, praying, engaging in religious singing/chanting, and reading sacred texts.

Religious/Social Conservatism is a seven-item measure reflecting: the student's degree of opposition to such things as casual sex and abortion, a belief that people who don't believe in God will be punished, and a propensity to use prayer as a means of seeking forgiveness. It also involves a commitment to proselytize and an inclination to see God as a father figure. (One might also label this measure as "fundamentalism.")

Religious Skepticism includes nine items reflecting beliefs such as "the universe arose by chance" and "in the future, science will be able to explain everything," and disbelief in the notion of life after death.

Religious Struggle includes nine items reflecting the extent to which the student feels unsettled about religious matters, disagrees with family about religious matters, feels distant from God, or has questioned her/his religious beliefs.

It should come as no surprise that some of these measures are related to each other (see the Appendix for a table of correlations among the ten measures). Thus, students who obtain high scores on Religious Commitment are also likely to obtain high scores on Religious Engagement and Religious/Social Conservatism, and low scores on Religious Skepticism. Thus, if a student is strongly committed to his or her religious faith, that student is also likely to engage frequently in prayer, to attend religious services regularly, and to hold conservative views on social issues. At the same time, that student is unlikely to express much religious skepticism.

Some of the measures of spirituality are also associated with one another, although the correlations are not as strong as in the case of the religious measures. Specifically, students who are on a spiritual quest also tend to express a strong ethic of caring and a strong ecumenical worldview. And students who demonstrate a high level of charitable involvement also tend to express a strong ethic of caring.

Religious Struggle does not show any substantial relationships with the other religious or spiritual measures, which means that students who are highly engaged in a religious struggle are not especially likely to score either high or low on any of the other measures.

Figure 2.1 portrays each of the ten measures as a circle. There are two clusters of measures: the five spirituality measures and four of the religiousness measures. The four religiousness measures show the most overlap with one another because these measures are more highly correlated with one another than are any of the other measures. The five measures of spirituality are also overlapping, but less so, indicating that they are not as highly correlated with one another as are the four religiousness measures. Finally, the measure of Religious Struggle stands by itself because it has only minimal correlations with the other nine measures. (Since the five spirituality measures are also moderately correlated with the other four religiousness measures, we could also show these two clusters as partially overlapping, but that would create a picture that would probably be too confusing.) See

Figure 2.1. The Ten Measures of Spirituality and Religiousness

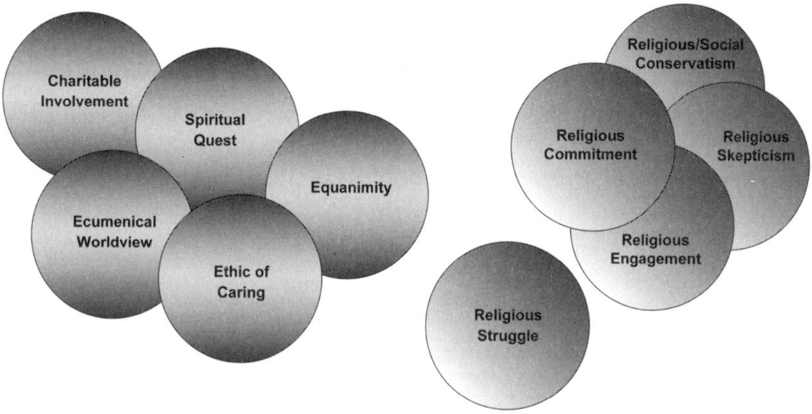

the Appendix (Table A.7) for a listing of all the correlations among these ten measures.

Taken together, these ten measures constitute a reasonably comprehensive set for assessing students' spiritual and religious qualities. Because we have minimized the use of terms such as "faith," "worship," and "God" and avoided the use of terminology that refers to particular religious belief systems (for example, "Jesus," "Buddha," "Koran"), the measures may be applicable to a wide variety of potential religious and nonreligious respondents. Despite these constraints, our measure of Religious Commitment appears to differentiate among traditional religious denominations, and in expected ways.[4] For example, the three most "committed" religious groups are Baptists, Mormons, and "other Christians" (mostly "nondenominational"), with more than 60 percent of the students belonging to each of these groups obtaining high scores on Religious Commitment. By contrast, the lowest percentages of high-scorers are found among Unitarian/Universalists (6%), Jews (5%), Buddhists (3%), and students who choose "none" as their religious preference (less than 1%). Roman Catholics and those who affiliate with mainstream Protestant denominations fall in between these two extremes, with between 24 percent and 37 percent receiving high scores.

DEFINING HIGH AND LOW SCORES ON MEASURES

Given that raw scores on scales such as these have no absolute meaning, how does one compare group differences in, say, average scores? How does one interpret changes in scores? A potentially useful way to contend with such interpretive challenges is to define high and low scores. In this way, it becomes possible to compare groups by determining what proportions of each group obtain high (or low) scores ("How do men and women compare in the proportion who score high on Equanimity?"). Similarly, we can more easily make meaning out of changes in scores over time by observing increases or decreases in the proportion of students who earn high (or low) scores ("How many of our current juniors score high on Spiritual Quest, compared to when they were freshmen?").

Since a student's score on one of our measures of spirituality or religiousness reflects the degree to which the student possesses the quality being measured, defining high or low scores is, to a certain extent, arbitrary. Nevertheless, we have tried to take a rational approach to such definitions by posing the following question: In order to defend the proposition that someone possesses a high (or low) degree of the trait in question, what *pattern* of responses to the entire set of questions that make up that scale would that person have to show? Our final definitions of high and low scores were quite stringent. For example, on the Equanimity scale, which is composed of five items, the respondent would have to give the strongest possible response on at least four of the five items to qualify as a high-scorer. By this yardstick, only 19 percent of the students scored high on Equanimity when they started college. For a more detailed description of the process we followed in defining high and low scores, see the Appendix.

MEASURES IN CONTEXT

While it is difficult to make direct comparisons between our ten measures and most of the measures developed by earlier investigators, because of substantial differences in survey design, some of our scales do share enough item content with earlier efforts to warrant brief mention of those efforts here. In particular, our Religious Commitment scale appears to share a good deal of content with Allport and Ross's (1967) Intrinsic Religious Orientation scale, which has been identified as perhaps the most widely used measure of religiousness in social science research. Religious Commitment also appears to share common elements with several other measures: Williams's (1999) Commitment scale, Seidlitz and colleagues' (2002) Spiritual Transcendence index, Hall and Edward's (2002) Awareness scale, MacDonald's (2000) Religiousness factor, and Underwood and Terisi's (2002) Daily Spiritual Experience scale.

Our Religious Engagement scale shares some item content with Levin's (1999) Private Religious Practices scale, MacDonald's (2000) Religiousness factor, and especially with Idler's (1999) Organizational Religiousness scale. The negative pole of Genia's (1991) Spiritual Experience index contains items that are similar to some of those in our Religious/Social Conservatism scale, while the positive pole in some respects resembles our Ecumenical Worldview scale. Finally, at least two earlier measures appear to contain elements of our Equanimity scale: Underwood and Terisi's (2002) Daily Spiritual Experience scale and MacDonald's Existential Well-being scale.

We should also mention that measures such as Ethic of Caring and Charitable Involvement appear to tap spiritual qualities that may be especially relevant to the goals of education. Beck (1986), for example, in arguing that spiritual development "should be a focus in the schools," includes "love" and a "caring approach to other people" as essential qualities of a spiritual person. Noddings (1984, 1989) similarly argues that the cultivation of caring ought to be a basic goal of education. She also points out two forms of caring: "caring-about," which resembles our Ethic of Caring measure, and "caring-for," which resembles our Charitable Involvement measure.

Finally, we note that our measures of spirituality appear to incorporate the two dimensions of spirituality proposed by Elkins and colleagues (1988): Mission in Life (our Spiritual Quest) and Altruism (our Charitable Involvement and Ethic of Caring). Further, in discussing altruism, Elkins and colleagues mention "a sense of . . . being part of a common humanity," which appears to relate directly to Ecumenical Worldview.

In the chapters that follow, these ten measures will frame our discussion of how students change spiritually and religiously during college, and how the college experience shapes students' spiritual development.

CHAPTER THREE

SPIRITUAL QUEST
The Search for Meaning and Purpose

Over the years, we have learned through our own and others' work a great deal about college students: who they are, what dreams they hold, what expectations they have, and how they experience life in college and beyond. Today, more than eleven million traditionally aged undergraduates bring with them to campuses across the country a wide range of talents, interests, aspirations, and expectations. Increasingly, they come from diverse racial, ethnic, socioeconomic, and religious backgrounds; their childhood and adolescent years are characterized by widely varying life circumstances and cultural traditions that frame— consciously or not—how they view themselves, others, and the world. And yet amidst all these differences and dimensions of potential divide, these students share many common hopes, concerns, passions, dreams, and responsibilities within the essence of their humanity. They also ask the same existential questions: Who am I? What is the meaning of life? What is my purpose? Who can—and will—I become?

These are, at heart, spiritual questions. Their answers are rooted in a lifelong, internal process of seeking personal authenticity; developing a greater sense of connectedness to self and others through relationship and community; deriving meaning, purpose, and direction in life; being open to exploring a relationship with a higher power that transcends human existence and knowing; and valuing the sacred. (These descriptions are extracted from definitions of spirituality proposed by Hill et al., 2000; Love and Talbot, 1999; and Zinnbauer, Pargament, and Scott, 1999.)

Spirituality can also be thought of as an animating, creative, ener-gizing, and meaning-making force—a "dynamic expression" of who we are. (These descriptions are taken from definitions of spirituality offered by Baker, 2003; Dyson, Cobb, and Forman, 1997; Goddard, 2000; Hindman, 2002; King, 1996; and Tanyi, 2002.) Some contend that although it may be manifest through highly variable personal mechanisms, spirituality is a biologically integral component of being human (see, for example, Narayanasamy, 1999; Stoll, 1989; Wright, 2000). It is the impetus that compels us to ask why we do what we do, pushes us to seek fundamentally better ways of doing it, and propels us to make a difference in the world (Zohar and Marshall, 2004). Within the spiritual domain, human development can be characterized both by one's capacity to integrate the many other aspects of development—cognitive, social, emotional, moral—with one's capacity for integrity, wholeness, openness, self-responsibility, and authentic self-transcendence (Helminiak, 1987).

CONCEPTUALIZING SPIRITUAL QUEST

Spiritual quest is a form of existential engagement that empha-sizes individual purpose and meaning-making in the world (Klaassen and McDonald, 2002). Fundamentally, spiritual quest represents the "seeking" in us that can lead to a better under-standing of who we are, why we are here, and how we can live a meaningful life—the "big" questions we all confront, often for the first time as young adults. Composed of nine items, the Spiritual Quest scale is the most process-oriented of our mea-sures. It reflects primarily an engagement in the search for meaning and purpose in life, underwritten by several key aspira-tions, including finding answers to the mysteries of life; seeking beauty in one's life; developing a meaningful philosophy of life; becoming a more loving person; attaining inner harmony; and attaining wisdom. Acknowledging that spiritual growth is facili-tated through interactions with others, the measure also consid-ers the number of students' close friends who are searching for meaning and purpose; and the frequency with which students talk with their friends about life's purpose and meaning. In short, the notion of an active "quest" is clearly suggested by words such as "searching," "developing," "finding," "seeking," "becoming," and "attaining."

In many ways, spiritual quest is at the core of spiritual development. Individual items in the Spiritual Quest scale speak to aspects of many of our other measures. "Attaining inner harmony," for example, has implications for dealing effectively with stress and maintaining a healthy perspective and capacity for resilience in the midst of life's inevitable trials and tribulations (Equanimity). Similarly, "becoming a more loving person" implies a commitment to caring for others and contributing to the welfare of the community (Ethic of Caring and Charitable Involvement) as well as to valuing the interconnectedness of life, embracing common elements of our human journeys, and respecting the differences among us that can provide texture and richness within our lives (Ecumenical Worldview). At the same time, "attaining wisdom" and "developing a meaningful philosophy of life" reflect the aims of many religious faiths (Religious Commitment, Religious Engagement), while working toward "finding answers to the mysteries of life" is often at the root of Religious Struggle.

We should understand and attend to college students' spiritual quest, for several reasons. How students perceive their position in the world, develop a sense of meaning and purpose in life, and seek inner harmony and self-awareness are all critical components of healthy identity development and mature psychological well-being. Earlier research has shown that those who view themselves as being on a spiritual quest tend to exhibit an active, open disposition toward tackling the perplexing issues that many individuals face when trying to establish their place and purpose in the world. Developing people's abilities to access, nurture, and give expression to the spiritual dimension of life impacts how they engage with the world and fosters within them a heightened sense of connectedness that promotes empathy, ethical behavior, civic responsibility, passion, and action for social justice (Allport and Ross, 1967; Batson, 1976; De Souza, 2003; Klaassen and McDonald, 2002).

An important distinction to be made is that a spiritual quest is not synonymous with being committed to a particular faith tradition or being otherwise settled in one's religious perspectives. Indeed, actively engaging in a spiritual quest may be a manifestation of several different religious orientations. For example, when we ask students to characterize their current beliefs, we find that those who are high-scorers on Spiritual Quest are three times more likely than low-scorers (36% vs. 12%) to report that they are "seeking," which points to the relative fluidity of their belief system. (As discussed in Chapter Two, distinctions made in this chapter regarding high- and low-scorers on the Quest measure—and on measures discussed in subsequent chapters—have been based on students' patterned responses to the items that compose the measure. See the Appendix for more detail.) At the same time, 19 percent of high-scorers, compared with only 12 percent of low-scorers, say they are "conflicted," which indicates that an element of religious conflict may be an underlying component of seeking among some of those who are more deeply engaged in questing. Similarly, slightly more high-scorers (11%) than low-scorers (9%) say that they are "doubting" their religious beliefs, which suggests that for some students, spiritual quest itself may be rooted in a fundamental examination of their religious faith. (This small difference is of borderline significance statistically: $p < .01$, $p > .001$. Henceforth only differences that exceed the .001 level of confidence will be reported. See the Appendix for more detail.)

In contrast, those who are high-scorers on Spiritual Quest are also more likely than their low-scoring peers to say they are "secure" in their religious beliefs (48% vs. 40%) and to report that they pray (39% vs. 15%) or meditate (10% vs. 1%) on a daily basis. These findings illustrate the variable, and sometimes complex, relationship between spiritual questing and religious conviction. Indeed, while religiosity may play a key role in the process by which individuals formulate responses to core questions of meaning and purpose, resolution of these concerns may result in deepening religiosity or, for some, perhaps, a rejection of it.

Our findings also show that students' inclinations toward spiritual questing may affect their motivation for attending college. For example, among freshmen who score high on Spiritual Quest, 71 percent indicate that "finding my purpose in life" is an "essential" or "very important" reason for them to go to college. Only 30 percent of low-scorers say this. Similar patterns are evident when comparing the percentages of high and low Spiritual Quest scorers who believe that it is "essential" or "very important" for their campus to enhance their self-understanding (90% of high-scorers vs. 41% of low-scorers); provide for their emotional development (85% vs. 38%); and encourage personal expression of spirituality (73% vs. 23%).

DEVELOPMENT OF SPIRITUAL QUEST DURING THE UNDERGRADUATE YEARS

At the end of their junior year in college, students are more inclined than they were as entering freshmen to rate "integrating spirituality in my life" as a "very important" or "essential" life goal (50%, compared with 42% as freshmen). Indeed, regardless of the type of campus students attend, one of the largest changes during the first three years of college occurs in students' propensity to engage in a spiritual quest. Overall, the number of students with high Spiritual Quest scores increases from 24 to 33 percent, and the number of students with low scores drops from 31 to 20 percent. Including those who score moderately on this scale, we find that by the end of their junior year, fully eight in ten undergraduates are at least moderately engaged in a spiritual quest.

Also noteworthy is that there is a good deal of change in individual students' propensity for spiritual questing. Specifically, only about half of the students (52%) obtain similar scores (high, medium, or low) at the two time points they were surveyed. Students whose score on this measure increases over the three-year period outnumber those whose score decreases by 2 to 1 (32% vs. 16%). Conclusively, students are twice as likely to show increases in Spiritual Quest than they are to show decreases.

Of the nine items contained in our Spiritual Quest scale, seven show higher scores among junior year respondents than among those same students three years earlier when they were entering freshmen, which tells us that for many young adults questions of meaning and purpose become increasingly more salient over the course of their undergraduate careers. The largest increases are observed in the number of students who rate the following life goals as either "very important" or "essential": developing a meaningful philosophy of life (55% of juniors vs. 41% of freshmen), seeking beauty in my life (66% vs. 54%), becoming a more loving person (83% vs. 67%), and attaining inner harmony (63% vs. 49%). Between these two time points, roughly one-third of students showed increases in the personal priority they place on attaining wisdom and in the number of their friends who are actively engaged in searching for meaning and purpose in life. In addition, approximately one-quarter of the students increased the priorities they assign to finding answers to the mysteries of life and searching for meaning and purpose in life. A similar increase was observed in the proportion reporting that they discuss the meaning of life with friends.

One student we interviewed, David (a pseudonym), offered a perspective on why inclinations toward spiritual questing may increase during college, which resonated well on many levels with the insights we heard from others: "I'm on a journey, a journey to self-discovery, but now I'm at the stage where I'm really trying to examine myself. I just turned twenty, and I've found that twenty is an interesting age. You're too young to be around the twenty-one-and-older crowd, but you're too old to be around the eighteen-and-under crowd. It's a very reflective age. It tends to be sort of like your alone-time age, and the questions that I'm starting to ask myself now are looking at more than just reflection. I'm looking at my future goals, and what it is that I want to have. What do I want to accomplish—not just academically, not just professionally, but really, personally, holistically? Right now, I'm sort of in the process of assessing and evaluating not just myself but those around me."

Asked to talk more about how he views his spiritual journey, David continued: "I really just want to get to a place where I feel like I know myself well enough to be able to make informed decisions, where I'm able to sort through life and do the things that I want to do. I just want to get to the place where I'm happy, spiritually sound, personally developed, and I think undergraduate education is the process where you're sort of laying the groundwork for that. You have to start somewhere. So although it may be a little rocky, a little contradictory, a little shaky now, I think that as you go through life, and as you get older, you're able to practice these skills that help you develop spiritually."

While David's sentiments tend to capture well the perspectives of many students we interviewed, there are also students for whom being on a spiritual quest does not resonate. The perspective of one woman reflects well the concern some students have about engaging too heavily in this realm: "I've kind of decided that I'm going to focus on school rather than myself. I think that with school comes learning and experiences that aren't anticipated. I think that if I try and find spirituality and go and seek it out, like maybe I have been, to find some greater meaning to my life and my purpose, that I'm going to spend so much time focused on that, and will be disappointed if I don't find anything."

As young adults search for their identity and learn about themselves through their relations with others, psychosocial support is crucial in helping them examine the questing dimension of their spirituality. Drawing meaning from their lives, they need to explore their place in the world and in their relationships to discover their individual selves and talents (Bruce and Cockreham, 2004; Gilligan, 1982; Verma and Santa Maria, 2006). Interactions with a diverse set of peers may motivate young adults to reflect on and develop a spiritual identity as they struggle to make meaning and find purpose in life, and college offers a relatively "safe" environment in which to explore that. As one student remarked, "On the college campus, there are so many different people coming together. Even though everyone is coming here from a different background—and they're probably headed somewhere completely different than everyone else when they graduate, and they're here to study different things—they're still all here to get a degree and to have their undergraduate experience. And so, while there are so many different perspectives and motivations that are all brought together, it's also empowering because while you can see all those different perspectives, you're also very connected to many different people."

For all its potential long-term benefits, the transition to college for many students can induce a state of disequilibrium or loss of synchrony that prompts them to reflect on issues of meaning and purpose, questions of character and identity, and their own perspectives on a potentially wide range of other issues that previously may not have been of any significant personal relevance. Other challenging life circumstances also commonly provide motivation to deepen one's connection with the transcendent (Crawford, O'Dougherty Wright, and Masten, 2006). For the students we surveyed and interviewed, traumatic events have indeed had an effect on their spiritual views, often serving to catalyze their search for meaning and purpose. For example, among students who had experienced the death of a close friend or family member while in college, 59 percent said that the experience had changed their spiritual and religious perspectives. In most cases (46%), the effect was "strengthening."

As one student explained, "Since coming to college, my life [has] changed a lot. I had a lot of big events. I moved. My dad passed away, and I had a grandmother who passed away within the same year. It was really like back-to-back-to-back, and it was a tough, tough time. Before, I was more focused on religion, but almost more religion for, like, the visual appearance to my family, not religion in my heart. I think now I'm trying to find it for myself, find what I believe for myself and what I want for myself. For me, spirituality is about becoming more aware of how many other ideas are out there, and how other people interpret those ideas and use them in living their own lives. It's become more of this kind of journey for me, in the sense of finding out what I believe and how I want to believe it, and what I feel is right for me, which is difficult and it's something I've just started doing."

Others shared similar stories of personal challenge and the ensuing dialogues with friends: "For me, it's interesting because conversations with my friends don't start with anything really spiritual. But, you know, when something bad happens, that's when you tend to talk about stuff, you know, a relationship ends or somebody's relative dies or somebody got severely injured or something. That's when this [spiritual] talk tends to come up with me and my friends."

DEMOGRAPHIC DIFFERENCES

As we noted earlier, the college-going population within the United States today is increasingly diverse, which means that our campus communities are made up of individuals who may prioritize the spiritual dimension of their lives very differently. To be sure, entire books could be written that focus solely on gender, religious faith, or other demographic group differences in spiritual and religious development. Our emphasis in this book is on how students *as a whole* tend to change during college and on what aspects of, and experiences within, the college environment tend to facilitate or hinder that change. However, we also address noteworthy demographic differences as they arise.

When we consider gender differences in inclination toward spiritual questing and engagement, for example, we find that women are more likely than men to be high-scorers on Spiritual Quest, both at the time they enter college (27% of women score high vs. 21% of men) and three years later (36% vs. 29%). While both men and women show between 8 and 9 percentage points of growth during college in the proportions who are high-scorers on Spiritual Quest, gendered patterns of change on selected items that compose the Spiritual Quest measure are markedly different. To illustrate, while there is a notable gap in the comparative value that freshman women and men place on becoming a more loving person (75% of freshman women rate this pursuit as "essential" or "very important" vs. 54% of freshman men), this gap narrows substantially during college (to 86% vs. 74% of female and male juniors, respectively) because men show nearly twice the increase of women.

Similarly, during college, men are much more likely than women are to increase the frequency with which they discuss the meaning of life with friends. By the third year of college, there is only a 2 percent difference between men and women when it comes to their involvement to at least "some" extent in these conversations (roughly 70% of both male and female juniors report at least "some" level of engagement). By comparison, at the time students entered college, the gender gap favored women by 10 percent. Finally, while the percentages of first-year male and female college students who place high value on developing a meaningful philosophy of life are nearly identical (40% of men vs. 41% of women rate this as "essential" or "very important"), by the time these students reach their junior year, men surpass women by a 4 percent margin (57% vs. 53%).

Interesting religious faith differences in the priority placed on spiritual quest are also evident. When they enter college,

Hindus and Mormons are more likely to be high-scorers on Spiritual Quest (53% and 54%, respectively) than their peers who adhere to other faith traditions. More than three in ten Buddhist, Islamic, Episcopalian, and Eastern Orthodox students also score high on Spiritual Quest. These higher-than-average inclinations toward spiritual questing persist during college, as reflected by the fact that three years later these same groups are still the most likely to score high on Spiritual Quest. Among students of other religious faiths, the largest increases over time in high-scorers on Spiritual Quest are evident among Baptists (29% are high-scorers as freshmen vs. 40% as juniors) and Catholics (22% vs. 35%). How particular aspects of these students' religious faiths may specifically serve to enhance quest inclinations warrants further focused study.

In sum, it appears that for many college students, increasingly active engagement in spiritual questing is a natural part of their young adult development. Upon entering college, some students exhibit strong inclinations toward spiritual questing; indeed, as addressed earlier in this chapter, their very motivations for attending college seem to touch on some of the key aspects of this measure. Major life events that occur during the course of their undergraduate years, such as the death of a close friend or family member, lead many students to intensify that quest; for others, such experiences may "weaken" their connection to spiritual aspects of their lives, at least temporarily. As addressed in the next section, we also find that other elements of the college experience and the choices students make during college have notable impacts on students' spiritual questing.

IMPACT OF COLLEGE ON STUDENTS' SPIRITUAL QUESTING

To test whether particular college experiences affect students' spiritual questing, we used statistical techniques that enable us to control for the potentially biasing effects of a wide range of other factors (see Appendix). In this way, we are able to efficiently sort through many potential variables to identify those that are the clearest, strongest predictors of growth or decline in spiritual questing during the first three years of college. Through these analyses, we learned that: interactions with faculty, selected academic courses of study and curricular experiences, working, and other personal practices that students may partake in during college play influential roles in shaping students' propensity toward spiritual questing.

FACULTY

Students whose professors encourage them to explore questions of meaning and purpose are inclined to show larger-than-average increases in their inclinations toward spiritual questing between their freshman and junior years, irrespective of their demographic characteristics, field of study, or the type of college or university (public, private, religiously affiliated, and so on) they attend. These effects can be potentially very powerful. Among those whose professors "frequently" encourage such exploration, there is a 14 percent increase in the number who score high on Spiritual Quest; those who report "occasional" encouragement show an 8 percent increase. By comparison, students who interact with faculty who are "not at all" inclined to encourage them to explore issues related to meaning and purpose show just a 6 percent increase. Similar effects are evident among students whose professors encourage their spiritual development. One explanation for these findings is that these practices may promote more integrated learning among students, helping them to recapture what Robert Nash (2008) has referred to as a "missing holism."

This kind of encouragement from professors, however, is more the exception than the rule in contemporary colleges and universities. Across all different types of campuses, most students (62%) report that their professors "never" encourage discussions of religious/spiritual matters, and only 20 percent report that their professors "frequently" encourage exploration of questions of meaning and purpose. Several juniors and seniors in our focus groups remarked that this was the first time since they enrolled in college that they had had an opportunity to discuss such issues with other students, and that they welcomed the opportunity, despite the fact that most of them told us that they were initially motivated to participate in the focus group primarily for the money rather than the advertised topic ("spirituality").

In contrast, one of the students we interviewed felt that the lack of encouragement to explore religious or spiritual issues is a "good thing because everybody has different views and beliefs" and resonated with the notion that "you shouldn't bring God up in an academic setting." Others, though, believe that addressing topics that could be perceived as being too closely linked with religion is "taboo," a view that contributed to the disconnect they perceive between their own personal and intellectual interests and their actual academic experiences. Students' observations on some of the prevailing assumptions within academe that we've discussed in the opening chapters were also highlighted in these conversations, including the "devaluing" of nonintellectual pursuits and what they perceived to be faculty members' tendency to dismiss as irrelevant anything that "can't be described scientifically or rationally."

The students with whom we spoke concurred unanimously that they were not receptive to being "told" by faculty what to think or believe in matters of meaning, purpose, and spirituality. Many also acknowledged that addressing the kinds of "internal stuff" that falls within the realm of students' quest for meaning and purpose can be very challenging. One woman who tried to imagine herself in her various professors' roles admitted that although she thinks it would be "great" if faculty did occasionally engage students in some of the broader topics, themes, and implications of their subject matter, she has "no idea" how she would go about stimulating those kinds of discussions and exchanges, particularly given some of the "sensitivities" that could come into play. Reflecting on how these conversations might be legitimized within academic contexts, another student commented, "I think the one thing I would change is professors. They're almost like ... scared ... they're going to offend somebody. I mean, it's rare that you get a professor to actually sit there and show you what they believe. I've never seen a professor actually involved in a real debate with students."

Interestingly, many students seem to presume that faculty members characteristically have little, if any, interest themselves in these matters and, by extension, this is why they don't encourage students to consider questions of meaning and purpose or otherwise support so-called spiritual aspects of students' development. Students also seemed to think that on the whole, those who pursue professorial careers are, in the words of one student, "not religious at all." In fact, findings from the faculty component of our study show that, for many faculty members, the spiritual dimension of life is highly relevant (Lindholm, Astin, and Astin, 2005). Within today's professoriate, four out of five faculty members describe themselves as "a spiritual person." Nearly half say they are spiritual "to a great extent." In addition, seven in ten faculty view "developing a meaningful philosophy of life" as an "essential" or "very important" life goal. A similar proportion say they "seek opportunities to grow spiritually" to at least "some" extent and that they engage in self-reflection to a "great" extent. Similarly, for nearly half of today's faculty, "integrating spirituality in my life" is "essential" or "very important." Faculty members are more inclined to describe themselves as "spiritual" than "religious." However, their students might be surprised to learn that, overall, more than three in five college professors (64%) say that they consider themselves to be "a religious person," either "to some extent" (29%) or "to a great extent" (35%). Only about one-third of faculty (37%) say they are "not at all" religious. In Chapter Nine, we address some of the challenges faculty face in addressing students' spiritual development, and we offer ideas for how those who might wish to engage students more holistically can do so.

CURRICULUM

Other academically related factors also contribute to growth in students' inclinations toward spiritual questing, including time spent doing homework and studying. While perhaps a somewhat puzzling association initially, this finding is replicated across a number of spiritual measures that will be addressed in subsequent chapters and seems to be most directly attributable to the broader importance of purposeful involvement. Indeed, we found that academic engagement—as reflected in the hours per week that a student commits to studying or doing homework—had a powerful positive predictive effect on the widest variety of college outcomes, ranging from retention to overall satisfaction with college to social activism (Astin, 1993).

Students who perform course-based community service also show larger-than-average gains in inclination toward spiritual questing. Over the past decade, the inclusion of service learning opportunities within traditional undergraduate curricula has gained in popularity. So-called service learning is a form of holistic, experiential education in which students actively address human and community needs while also engaging in purposefully designed activities that facilitate student learning and development. Key components of the experience are reflection and reciprocity, and its benefits include helping students to do the following: identify and direct their personal goals through exploration of moral and ethical positions about themselves and their communities; relate larger social issues to their own lives; prepare for participating in a democracy as an informed citizen; and link service with academic coursework by enabling them to test otherwise abstract theory in the "real world" and giving community service an "intellectual underpinning" (Astin et al., 2000; Jacoby and Associates, 1996; Lott et al., 1997; McClam et al., 2008; Sax and Astin, 1997). The students in our study who participated in service learning over the three years showed an 11 percent increase in representation among high-scorers on Spiritual Quest, relative to a 7 percent increase among those who had no such participation.

We also find differences in spiritual questing based on students' course of study. These differences are present when students enter college and tend to persist throughout their undergraduate careers. For example, freshmen who plan to major (or who end up majoring as juniors) in the health professions or in the fine arts or humanities tend to show comparatively greater quest inclinations relative to their peers who are interested in other fields. By contrast, those who pursue studies in the physical sciences, computer science, or business show below-average levels of engagement in spiritual questing. These findings suggest that students who are drawn to certain areas of study may be at least somewhat predisposed toward high (or low) engagement in spiritual questing. Related developmental and practical implications warrant further study.

Changes in quest inclinations follow a similar pattern. Thus, majoring in the health professions heightens, or intensifies, students' propensity to engage in a spiritual quest, while majoring in mathematics or statistics, history or political science, or engineering has a dampening effect on students' quest inclinations. These differential changes by major field could well be peer-group effects, where the individual student, over time, tends to conform to the dominant values and inclinations of the peer group. However, our data suggest that faculty may also play a role in these changes, because when we pose to faculty the question of whether colleges should attend to facilitating students' spiritual development, we find substantial differences in responses based on their academic field. The highest levels of faculty agreement with the notion that colleges should be involved in facilitating students' spiritual development are found in the health sciences, and the lowest levels are in the biological sciences, social sciences, physical sciences, and agriculture/forestry.

PERSONAL PRACTICES AND OTHER EXPERIENCES

Engaging in selected personal practices during the first three years of college also impacts students' Spiritual Quest scores. In particular, engaging regularly in self-reflection shows a substantial positive effect on spiritual questing. Figure 3.1 illustrates this effect by comparing students who seldom or never engage in self-reflection (once a month or less—the bottom line in the figure) with two other groups of students: those who engage in self-reflection on a daily basis (the top line in the figure), and those who do a moderate amount of self-reflection (one or more times per week, but not daily—the middle line in the figure). Students who self-reflect on a daily basis during college show a much greater-than-average increase of 18 percent in high-scorers for Spiritual Quest, while those who seldom or never self-reflect actually show a decline of 4 percent in high-scorers. Students who do a moderate amount of self-reflection score in between, with a 7 percent increase in high-scorers during the first three years of college. A similar pattern of effects was found to be associated with meditation.

The 2004 (freshman) figures actually reveal a good deal of *self-selection*, meaning that as entering freshmen, the students who will ultimately end up doing the most self-reflection during college (top line) already have the highest initial Spiritual Quest scores

FIGURE 3.1. FREQUENCY OF SELF-REFLECTION AND SPIRITUAL QUEST

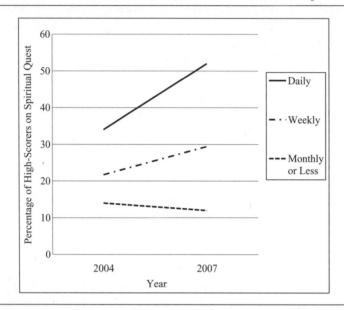

(34% high-scorers) when they enter college, while students who will end up doing the least self-reflection while in college (bottom line) have the lowest initial scores (16% high-scorers). Such a self-selection bias underscores the need to study *changes* in Spiritual Quest (between 2004 and 2007) rather than merely comparing 2007 (junior) scores with how much self-reflection students engage in after they enter college.

Time spent critically contemplating one's perceptions, experiences, and roles may help individuals gain greater awareness and self-understanding, and help resolve disconnections between one's values and experiences (Ash and Clayton, 2004; Hatcher and Bringle, 1997; Morton, 1993). Through these processes, students can better embrace their capacity to develop and articulate their own understanding of the world and their place within it.

Other positive influences on students' quest development include several activities that would be expected to stimulate their interest in exploring spiritual and religious matters: reading sacred texts, reading other material on spirituality and religion, and discussing religion. A woman we interviewed who had recently taken a class that "required reading the Bible as a piece of litera-ture, rather than as a spiritual guide" offered her perspective on how these types of activities might function to enhance spiritual questing: "It was a totally new and different experience that helped me to view religion from a different standpoint and forced me to think about my faith/spirituality and religious affiliation with a critical mind. It forced me to question my faith and come to an understanding of what I do and do not believe."

Helping friends with personal problems also promotes spiri-tual questing. The pattern of results is strikingly similar to the pattern for self-reflection already shown in Figure 3.1. Among students who help friends with personal problems at least "occa-sionally," there is a 6 percent point gain in high-scorers on Spiritual Quest. For those who "frequently" help their friends with personal problems, the gain is even larger (11%). By comparison, among those students who say they do not get involved helping friends with their problems, a 6 percent decline is evident in high-scorers on Spiritual Quest between the freshman and junior years. One woman's reflections on the value of friendships underscore the importance that close relationships with others can play, both in helping us to better understand ourselves and in supporting our quest to grow spiritually: "Developing a strong relationship with my freshman year roommate and new best friend was very mean-ingful. It was amazing to be put in a room with a 'random' stranger and be able to develop such a strong bond of mutual trust, admiration, and love. She has helped me in many ways by always listening, giving advice, and allowing me to freely express myself without passing any judgment."

A young man shared similar thoughts: "My roommate is very honest and open, and he helped me through some major situa-tions. We are able to challenge one another with goals for our spiritual lives, as well as everyday life." Desire to help others is also illustrated by another measure we included in our analyses, "donating money to charity," which is also positively predictive of enhanced spiritual questing during college.

At this juncture it should be pointed out that a pattern is emerging with respect to some of the activities that have been found to promote spiritual questing. Specifically, three of the activities that have been shown to have positive effects on the student's inclination to engage in a spiritual quest—engaging in community service, helping friends with personal problems, and donating money to charity—are all forms of "charitable involvement," a spiritual quality that will be discussed at length in chapter Five.

Students who work for pay also show greater gains in Spiritual Quest scores than do their nonemployed peers. Insight as to reasons for this effect is provided by the reflections of one student who viewed "working" as one of the most meaningful experiences she has had while in college: "Working gave me a look into what real responsibility is like, and what working with colleagues post-college will feel like. We had to debate and discuss every business matter, and what we did really impacted the business, our funds, and as a result, our paychecks. This taught me to speak my mind, be blunt but not hurtful, and work with others to complete complex tasks."

IMPEDIMENTS TO SPIRITUAL QUESTING

Through our conversations with students in both individual and group settings, it became readily apparent that one of the greatest—if not the greatest—impediments to students' thoughtful exploration of life's so-called big questions are time pressures. One student we spoke with, Annette, described a process where she emerged from an "unhealthy" lifestyle of packing every minute of her college day with activities, to one that has become, over time, more balanced.

Annette is an international studies major at a small Christian liberal arts college in California. She pursues living life to the fullest. During her freshman year, Annette's schedule included running track, working in the volunteer center, and carrying eighteen units of coursework, all of which left her "completely physically, emotionally, mentally, spiritually exhausted." In describing her freshman routine, she said: "I would wake up every day, go to class, go to practice from 2 to 6 p.m. every day, do homework until early in the morning, sleep three, four hours, and do it all again the next day. There was no time for me to sit and think about things and ask, 'Well, what does this mean?'"

When presented with the opportunity to spend a semester in Europe in a study-abroad program, she saw a chance to give herself a break that, in retrospect, she deems as "the best experience" of her life thus far: "I wasn't practicing four hours a day. I wasn't killing myself in school. And it made me reevaluate my priorities. It doesn't necessarily matter, all the things you're doing—especially people at our school who are trying to validate themselves with their activities and achievements—when you can just be there, instead of doing things all the time. I think that helped a lot: just taking the time to be somewhere else. I think there's something about being out of your element and really finding God in other places." Clearly, Annette's semester abroad provided a break from the frenetic pace of her campus life that enabled her to engage in self-reflection.

After recovering from "commitment overflow" as a freshman, and enjoying a great experience overseas as a sophomore, Annette describes her junior year as a time when she began to sort out her big questions in life. From Annette's vantage point, it wasn't until she had a break from her busy schedule that she was able even to begin to consider dealing with these issues. In this way, rest, balance, and spirituality all became intertwined. These big questions in life are what she perceives as a common thread for juniors, who are realizing that the rest of their lives are just around the corner. She describes these questions as: "What am I going to do with my life? Why has God put me here, and why has God put these people in my life? Or, 'What's going on?' Why is everything so chaotic? I find myself having spiritual conversations a lot. It's interesting because, a lot of times, it's with people who aren't involved in any type of ministry on campus or any type of faith, and they want to ask me—especially people who knew me before I went overseas—'Well, what has changed? Why do you believe so much now?'"

Although campus life for Annette after her return from studying abroad has given her the opportunity to wrestle more consciously with these questions, she admits that familiar stresses have also reemerged. Like many others we interviewed, Annette describes the tensions she experiences within the hustle and bustle of what she characterizes as a more "individualistic" California lifestyle, relative to the more "collective" culture she experienced in Europe. When she feels a need to rest and regain the comparatively healthier balance she learned to achieve while living overseas, she detaches completely from her phone and computer and resorts to spending quiet time writing in her journal or having conversations with family members or mentors, a self-induced process she calls "detox." Thus, in spite of the continuing hectic pace of her college life, Annette is able to continue her spiritual quest because she now understands her need to make time for self-reflection.

Another student offers additional perspective on the "busy-ness" many students experience during their undergraduate years: "Even though I ask these questions, or as I talk to God on a regular basis, it's like there are still parts of me that I don't explore all the way because I say, 'Okay, now I have to go study' or 'Now I have to do this,' you know, just to get my mind off it. At the end of the day, I don't have time to dwell and say, 'Hmmm.' Never slowing down and taking the time out to explore your inner being and your inner self is a very dangerous thing, I think. And I didn't realize it until [the campus reverend] said something about, 'Busyness is an excuse.' It kind of made me say, 'Okay, uh-oh, what am I doing about my life, and how can I change it?'"

When asked to explain why she used the word "dangerous" in talking about not allowing yourself the time to reflect on life's bigger questions, this student mentions the potential perils of getting caught up in doing what you "should" be doing, simply because at some point it was what you decided or promised others you would do, or, as she has also sometimes felt, because it is too emotionally painful to make yourself think through alternatives: "If you just continue to live day to day, just moving through the motions, not really taking time out for yourself, and just doing what you think you're supposed to be doing, you don't take the time out to explore yourself. You don't take the time to say, 'Okay, well, I really don't feel like this may be right for me.' Instead of questioning that, you continue on with it. It's dangerous because there may be another path for you that you don't even know about, because you're so busy on this one path. Or there may be someone out there that you're supposed to be meeting, but you're so busy on this path that you can't even see it. It's dangerous because [that mind-set] doesn't let you really explore your life and live your life to the fullest. It's allowing you to live the life that's comfortable for you."

Another student who participated in one of our focus group interviews at a large Eastern public university offers a similar perspective: "A lot of times, I find myself wondering why we're in class, why we're in school, why I want to have a job, when it doesn't feel like I'm actually living. What would I have accomplished if I died tomorrow, after going to school for three years? Just going through it? And there are a lot of times when I'll opt to stay in and study or do something toward my career, as opposed to actually living and spending time with my family and friends. I feel like sometimes I miss out on connections because I'm too busy, like getting all wrapped up in society and the world I'm supposed to live in, my culture, and all the junk that I'm supposed to get done before I graduate, when I feel like I should really be spending my time with my friends, or just making connections."

Indeed, many of the students we interviewed talk about their struggle with finding a balance between attending sufficiently to all the things they "have" to do, while still preserving much-needed, and desired, time both for connecting with others and spending relaxing, quiet time alone; many of these same concerns are expressed by faculty, particularly young professors. As one remarks, "It's highly unrealistic that I'm going to find time to attend to my own spiritual needs until after I'm tenured." These sentiments from both students and faculty raise important questions about contemporary life, both within the academy and beyond.

SUMMARY

Our Spiritual Quest measure represents students' involvement in the inner process of seeking answers to who we are, why we are here, and how we can live a meaningful life. Through this study, we've seen that this dimension of life is highly relevant for a majority of students, and that while overinvolvement in the busyness of campus life can interfere with the student's efforts to pursue a spiritual quest, selected college activities can facilitate quest inclinations. A large enough number of students are able to participate in these activities so that over the course of their undergraduate careers, students generally tend to become more actively engaged in a spiritual quest. Students who show the largest increases in questing include not only those who regularly engage in self-reflection or meditation but also those whose professors either encourage them to explore questions of meaning and purpose or otherwise support students' spiritual development. Additional positive effects on questing are associated with majoring in selected fields and with being highly engaged academically. Another set of positive experiences includes various forms of "charitable involvement." Service learning courses, for example, provide fruitful opportunities for students to expand their spiritual quest, as does helping friends with personal problems and donating money to charity. Still another set of experiences that promote spiritual questing includes various forms of "religious engagement," working while attending college, as well as reading literature and having discussions, both of which provide students with a context to critically explore the inner dimensions of life.

It is also noteworthy that students on a spiritual quest often view their place in the world and their relationship to others by embodying a number of qualities that are found in other measures of this study. Those who scored high on Spiritual Quest also tended to exemplify an "ethic of caring," a commitment to values such as helping others in difficulty, working to reduce pain and suffering in the world, and looking to make the world a better place. They also possessed an "ecumenical worldview," characterized by an interest in understanding different religious traditions, as well as other countries and cultures, and holding a belief that love is at the root of all the great religions. Finally, they demonstrated a sense of "equanimity," a feeling of peace and centeredness, being able to find meaning in times of hardship, and a sense of a strong connection to all of humanity. These dimensions of spirituality are addressed in detail in the chapters that follow.

CHAPTER FOUR

EQUANIMITY

In preparing for this study, our project team engaged in an extended series of discussions concerning the concept of "spirituality," its meaning, and its role in higher education. We eventually reached a point where we agreed that one potentially useful approach to the definitional problem would be to describe what a "spiritual" person or a person who is "highly developed spiritually" would be like. When we asked ourselves what qualities such a person would likely display, one of the first constructs that came to mind was "equanimity." We weren't sure how such a quality might be measured or even whether it was possible to develop a measure of it, but we were convinced that equanimity was something that highly spiritual people were likely to exhibit.

One of our key findings is that students' sense of equanimity, like spiritual quest, shows significant growth during the college years.

In trying to understand a complex and somewhat abstract quality like equanimity, it can sometimes be helpful to bring to mind actual people who personify that quality. One contemporary exemplar of equanimity who comes immediately to mind is the Dalai Lama, the exiled religious leader of Tibet. While the Dalai Lama almost always seems to exhibit great wisdom, honesty, curiosity, and wit, we believe that most people who have heard this man speak or have spent any time with him are immediately struck by his calmness, serenity, centeredness, and seeming imperturbability. Considering that from a very early age the Dalai Lama has spent countless hours in contemplation and deep meditation, it comes as no surprise that our data show that students are most likely to develop a sense of equanimity if they engage frequently in self-reflection or meditation.

Measuring Equanimity

The Equanimity scale that emerged from our analysis of students' responses to the 2003 pilot survey comprised five items. Two of the five items begin the same: Since entering college, how often have you

- been able to find meaning in times of hardship?
- felt at peace, centered?

Response options included "frequently," "occasionally," and "not at all." The other three items in the Equanimity scale were preceded by "Indicate the extent to which each of the following describes you":

- I feel good about the direction in which my life is headed.
- I see each day, good or bad, as a gift.
- I am thankful for all that has happened to me.

Response options included "to a great extent," "to some extent," and "not at all."

The first item—finding meaning in times of hardship—perhaps more than any of the other four, captures the traditional dictionary meaning of "equanimity," which typically refers to one's capacity to "see the silver lining" during difficult or trying times. Most of the other statements suggest a general sense of psychological or spiritual well-being and optimism, coupled with a demeanor reflecting composure and calm. In spiritual or religious terms, we might describe a person who strongly endorses all five statements as one who experiences life as a "state of grace." From still another perspective, the five Equanimity items appear to capture some of the qualities that one associates with higher states of consciousness: a sense of calm, peacefulness, centeredness, and perhaps most important, self-transcendence, the ability to rise above or move beyond the limits of personal experience.

Note that "equanimity," as defined by statements such as these, also has a substantial affective component: feeling "at peace," feeling "good." There is also the suggestion of subtle affective states (peacefulness, calm, acceptance of things as they are) in words such as "gift," "thankful," and "find meaning."

We are not suggesting, however, that people who display a high level of equanimity never experience emotional conflicts. Indeed, the Dalai Lama often speaks and writes about the anger that he has felt in the face of the invasion and occupation of his home country by the Chinese government, and of the ways in which he has attempted to channel this anger in productive ways. It is probably the quality of equanimity that enables the Dalai Lama to pause, reflect, and redirect his emotional energy in this manner.

Research suggests that many other spiritual leaders are also able to function as effective social activists because of their highly developed sense of equanimity. Perhaps not all activists feel "centered" or "at peace," but it is clear that those who speak of spirituality as central to their lives in fact do (see Daloz et al., 1996). Other contemporary exemplars of equanimity who come to mind include South Africa's Nelson Mandela and Desmond Tutu, who led their country's liberation from apartheid; Jimmy Carter, the mediator of the Camp David Peace Accords (Brinkley, 1998); and Coretta Scott King, who has worked to carry on the legacy of her late husband (King, 1993). All of these leaders, except King, were, like the Dalai Lama, honored with the Nobel Peace Prize, and King had worked closely with her husband, Martin Luther King Jr., at the time he was awarded the prize. The biographers of such people have observed that they, like the Dalai Lama, all exhibit the qualities of calm and wisdom under pressure and are able to "find meaning in times of hardship."

To observe the actions of such exemplars not only suggests what mature equanimity might look like but also serves to underscore what it is not. For example, a casual reading of the five defining statements (above) might tempt one to equate "feeling at peace/centered" or "seeing each day, good or bad, as a gift" with complacency, placidity, passivity, or denial in times of adversity. These exemplars were obviously neither passive nor in denial about the adversities that motivated them to become activists. We hasten to add, however, that while equanimity can certainly be accompanied by activism, it is a very different thing. We would argue instead that the peace and calm typically associated with equanimity *allow* the person to channel anger or frustration into positive action. One is reminded here of the Eastern concept of "equal vision," the capacity to weigh contradictory or conflicting ideas, emotions, or events and to find commonalities (Mann, 1984). Equal vision has been described as "the attempt to perceive the same divine presence in all beings" (Omkarananda, 1999). People like Nelson Mandela and the Dalai Lama were clearly angry and frustrated with what was happening in their home countries, but it was their sense of equanimity that enabled them to act upon these powerful emotions with dignity, determination, logic, and passion.

While some of our exemplars may be more inclined than others to be "thankful for all that has happened," all with the exception of Mandela are associated in significant ways with religion, while Mandela's autobiography (1994) reveals a man with an extraordinarily rich interior life. So it comes as little surprise that our Equanimity measure shows positive associations, not just with our other measures of spirituality but also with measures of religiousness.[1]

While it may be difficult to imagine that our exemplars have all consistently "felt good" about the directions in which their lives have headed, all have rebounded from significant setbacks, indicating a capacity to find ways to reset their lives on courses that they could feel good about. Each of them lives and works from a sense of calling that might best be described as "authentic"; few people would question their sincerity. Those who have known our exemplars personally speak of their "presence," of the sense that they are able to be fully engaged with all they encounter. We might see the seeds of such a sense of mature "presence" in the feeling of "seeing each day, good or bad, as a gift."

EQUANIMITY IN COLLEGE STUDENTS

The Equanimity scale shows a number of interesting associations with various aspects of the student's college experience. For example, students with high Equanimity scores, compared to those with lower scores, tend to get better grades in college, report higher levels of psychological well-being, and be more satisfied with their overall college experience. And consistent with what we have already said about our exemplars, students with high Equanimity scores are also more likely than lower-scoring students to say that they want to "improve the human condition," "become a community leader," "become a more loving person," and "reduce pain and suffering in the world."

As entering freshmen, 19 percent of the students obtain high scores on the Equanimity scale. (Since all five Equanimity items had three response options [scored 3, 2, and 1], the highest possible score was 3×5, or 15. A student was considered to be high on Equanimity if her responses to the five items summed to either 14 or 15. This means that to qualify as a high-scorer the student had to give the highest response ["frequently" or "to a great extent"] on at least four of the five items, the middle response ["occasionally" or "to some extent"] on no more than one item, and the lowest response ["not at all"] on no items. Students with scale scores of 9 or lower were considered low-scorers on Equanimity.) By the time they reach the end of their junior year, this figure increases to 23 percent. (The number of low-scorers declines from 17 to 13 percent during the same period.) We see then that equanimity, like spiritual questing, grows during the college years. Examining how students' responses to the individual Equanimity items change, we find increases on four of the five items in the percentage giving the highest response ("frequently" or "to a great extent"), with the largest increase—from 52 to 61 percent—occurring in "being thankful for all that has happened to me." The next-largest increases occur with "being able to find meaning in times of hardship" (from 26% to 31%) and "seeing each day, good or bad, as a gift" (from 39% to 45%). The only item showing a net decrease is "felt at peace/centered," with the number of high-responders declining slightly from 32 to 29 percent. All five items, however, showed a decrease in the number of students giving the lowest response ("not at all").

This positive growth in equanimity is particularly remarkable in light of the finding that students' sense of psychological well-being shows a substantial decline during college (see Chapter Eight). The fact that our measure of psychological well-being contains items such as "felt that [my] life is filled with stress and anxiety" and "felt depressed" may help to explain why students' endorsement of one Equanimity item—"felt at peace/centered"—showed a slight decline during college. Given the positive association between these two scales, the growth in students' sense of equanimity would probably have been even greater if it weren't for the decline in their level of psychological well-being.

FACILITATORS OF EQUANIMITY

Students' sense of equanimity is most likely to strengthen during college if they engage in "inner work"—meditation, prayer, or self-reflection. About one college student in six meditates at least several times a week, compared to more than half who never meditate. When we compare these two groups in how their Equanimity scores change during college, we find an 8 percent increase in the number of high-scorers among those who meditate frequently, compared to only a 3 percent increase among those who never meditate. Self-reflection and prayer show similar patterns. College students who pray every day show a 7 percent increase in high-scorers on Equanimity, compared to only a 2 percent increase among those who never pray. Among students who engage in self-reflection on a daily basis there is also a 7 percent increase in high-scorers, compared to a 1 percent decline in high-scorers among those who never engage in self-reflection.

A compelling example of how self-reflection can promote equanimity is provided by one of our student interviewees: "The first class I actually took was field botany; we'd learn about plants and trees and stuff and then we'd take nature walks and we'd actually go out there and just look at them. And so in the midst of this stressful, you know, trying-to-fit-in-and-adjust college semester I had when I first got here, being able to just go out and—I know it sounds corny—but go out in nature and just accept everything for what it is, has been really powerful. I really, really loved that experience. I've taken a land use class in the Geography Department and a geology class where we've gone out, and there are a lot of trails. It's peaceful. I've gotten to know the trails really well from taking these classes. It's nice to have a place to be able

to go to on a walk and just sit on a bench and look out over the
ravine and just kind of chill when I need to. It's my secret place.
I go there to reflect; whether it's drama between people or being
frustrated with your schoolwork or issues at home, or you know,
I guess normal things that a college student would usually stress
out about. Sometimes I bring my journal to write. Other times I'll
just sit and look around and listen to the birds and squirrels and
the creek. After I come back I feel rejuvenated. I think that it's
easy to get fed up or distracted with small things, and being able
to go out there and let it all [hang] loose is really humbling. It
grounds me, and so I'm able to refocus and feel like I understand
where I fit in this world. It gives me a perspective on what is
important and what isn't. And so I'm able to come back and let
the small stuff go."

A similar story about the effects of meditation and yoga on
equanimity comes from a woman attending a Catholic university:
"We would meditate before we would do yoga, and after. And
when we would meditate, the point was to clear your mind of past
and future ideas, and just think about the present; once we have
that state of mind, then we do yoga. The yoga that I like to do
is more just stretching so that your body feels good. I've become
more flexible and feel calmer, and I've definitely noticed this
quarter, when I am usually stressed out, I just take a moment and
do some [yoga] salutations, and stay calm and then I can get
through it better. And sometimes I'm not stressed when I ought
to be, but it's because I'm already calm. With yoga, I feel a physical and a mental calmness and I focus on my spirituality. I don't
have to think as much. I let all the worries and negative things go
out of my mind, and then I feel at peace."

One of the advantages of interviews and focus groups is that
they provide insights about specific things that might not have
been anticipated when the survey questionnaire was designed.
When we asked a female student what most gets her in touch with
her sense of spirituality, here is what she told us: "I would say my
dancing. I've been dancing for over sixteen years now, but it
wasn't until I came to college that I started doing this kind of
dance called 'mime.' It is a lot of moving with your hands and
trying to imitate the words that are being said throughout the
music. I found myself being more connected. You have to listen

to a song over and over in order to know exactly every word that the person's saying, not to imitate every word, but to emulate what they're saying. I feel like that has definitely allowed me to reflect more within myself, and look at the song and apply it to my life, and use it to kind of get closer to God, and see exactly what He wants from me. For example, there's a song that I was getting ready to teach yesterday called, 'I Trust You.' It's talking about how basically even in the roughest of times, no matter what, 'I'll still come to you, I'll still trust in you, God, because I know that you'll see me through, that you'll help me.' And I found myself listening to the song over and over and really feeling like that's what I need to do. I need to trust and know that everything will be okay. So, my dancing is a place where I feel most connected."

Dance, of course, has long been employed as a meditative technique, because it effectively quiets the verbal mind and enables the individual to move beyond patterned responses. It's interesting to note that here the student is showing us how dance contributes to her sense of equanimity.

Another student enrolled in a religiously affiliated university explains how reflection, combined with a strong religious faith, enables him to maintain some sense of equanimity in the face of the many stresses of being a college student: "I find that I'm able to care about and love people around me better if I have a relationship with God first; it is a constant, and it's not something that ever fades. It only grows, and when you have that it makes loving everyone else around you a lot easier. Also, I find peace. Specifically at [my university], a lot of kids get overinvolved. For myself, I can say that I'm stretched in a million directions. But it's that quiet time, whether it's by myself or during a Bible study or when I'm in chapel, and afterwards, I write in my journal and reflect. Those are the times that God speaks to me. And those are the times that I feel at ease and as though I can just let it all go and focus."

Over the centuries meditation and reflection have been recommended by many different religious, philosophical, and therapeutic traditions as techniques not only for "calming" the mind but also for "getting to know" the mind. The possible effects of such inner work on equanimity may well be reflected in external behaviors such as composure and calmness, but it is also possible to think about a connection in terms of psychological processes.

One of the central goals of meditation, self-reflection, and other contemplative practices is to enhance self-awareness, that is, to "know thyself" at a deeper level, to be aware of various emotional states as they arise, and to have some understanding of the personal beliefs and life situations that are likely to elicit these states. Enhanced self-awareness, in turn, would likely contribute to the development of equanimity, since it enables the individual to devise alternatives to the reflexive "fight or flight" reaction that typically arises in response to adversity. The biographies of our exemplars, for example, suggest a critical role for "pause and reframing," a process whereby the self-aware individual is able to (1) recognize an intense emotional response to a negative life event, (2) pause and reframe the situation, and (3) channel the emotional energy in constructive ways. Self-awareness, of course, is the critical prerequisite condition for such a reframing process, since it enables one to recognize powerful emotional states as they arise, rather than simply act on them.

Another way of looking at the process of pause and reframing is that it represents a form of meaning-making. In one of the most widely read books of the past fifty years, *Man's Search for Meaning*, the late psychiatrist Viktor Frankl (1984) recounts his experience trying to survive in a Nazi death camp. His reflection on his attempts to maintain his humanity when its qualities were most under siege led him to develop an existential therapeutic approach founded on the assumption that making meaning is what makes us human. Most of his work with his patients involved supporting them in the search for the "silver lining," the meaning they could find in their suffering that would enable them to reframe their situation and persist with their lives. This approach was never about denying or masking but about locating the touchstone of possibility that created fresh meaning. In a sense, what Frankl discovered was that "being able to make meaning in times of hardship" provides the clearest evidence that the quest for meaning lies at the heart of the human spirit. In short, equanimity involves the capacity to frame and reframe meaning under stress while maintaining a sense of composure and centeredness.

College students too can experience moments of crisis during their undergraduate years. Although the college campus environment may seem insulated from the outside world, many students find themselves faced with life-altering situations like a death in the family, a separation or divorce of their parents, serious mental or physical health problems, or a variety of other personal challenges. Responding to such crises with equanimity can sometimes be facilitated if students are able to rely on practices like prayer, meditation, and self-reflection to help them navigate through these circumstances. For example, one student at a private Evangelical college received tragic news that his older brother had been in a serious accident and may have been paralyzed. When receiving this news, he said, "that was probably one of the first times that I could recognize how immediately I just prayed for stillness, and I got stillness. And that was my first response. I really do feel like my spirituality is something I get strength from."

Consistent with these findings on the positive effects of inner work, our data also show that equanimity can be enhanced by reading sacred texts and especially by "other reading" on the subjects of religion or spirituality.

Another type of experience that appears to enhance equanimity is involvement in charitable activities. In fact, our survey data show that most of the specific activities that make up the Charitable Involvement scale—doing volunteer work, helping friends with personal problems, and donating money to charity—contribute to the growth of equanimity during the college years. (These same activities were also shown to enhance spiritual questing; see Chapter Three.) Among students who frequently help friends with personal problems during college, there is a 7 percent increase in the number who score high on Equanimity, compared to a 2 percent decrease among students who help friends only occasionally. Similar patterns of change in equanimity are associated with doing volunteer work and donating money to charity.

That involvement in charitable activities during college should contribute to students' equanimity is not surprising, given the abundant evidence showing that participation in community service promotes growth in personal attributes such as self-esteem, critical thinking skills, commitment to serving others, interpersonal skills, conflict resolution skills, and social self-confidence (Astin, 1996; Astin and Sax, 1998; Astin, Sax, and Avalos, 1999; Astin and Vogelgesang, 2006; Vogelgesang and Astin, 2000). It should also be noted that a well-designed community service experience typically involves a good deal of self-reflection (Giles and Eyler, 1994), a process that, as we have already seen, enhances growth in equanimity. Such an interpretation may also help to explain the fact that equanimity is also strengthened by experiences such as study abroad, going on a religious mission trip, and interacting with people from different racial groups. Such activities, which inevitably expose students to people who are different from themselves, may well encourage them to engage in self-reflection.

Equanimity is also strengthened by three other student activities: leadership training, student clubs and groups, and group projects organized as part of a class. Keeping in mind the positive effects of community service and helping friends with personal problems, we can begin to see a pattern emerging: *equanimity appears to be enhanced by engaging in group activities that have constructive ends.* This conclusion is consistent with still another finding: that growth in equanimity is greater than average among students who major in one of the allied health fields (nursing, physical therapy, and so on).

We were somewhat surprised to find that students' sense of equanimity can also be strengthened by their participation in intercollegiate football or basketball, the so-called revenue sports. Among students who are members of such teams—about 6 percent of our sample—there is a 15 percent increase in high-scorers on Equanimity during college, compared to an increase of only 3 percent among the remaining 94 percent of our students. A possible explanation for this effect has to do with the fact that many teams take on a quasi-religious fervor, as team members may participate in group prayer before, during, and after games. At the same time, these teams have increasingly come to rely on sports psychology, which emphasizes relaxation, "centering," and other elements of "positive psychology." Such group activities, practiced over the course of a season, may well contribute to the development of equanimity. One is also reminded here of the Los Angeles Lakers professional basketball team, whose enigmatic coach, longtime Zen practitioner Phil Jackson, asks his players to meditate before each game.

Another somewhat unexpected finding is that growth in equanimity during college is positively associated with how much students study (another experience that appears to promote spiritual questing; see Chapter Three). Among students who study more than fifteen hours per week, we observe a 7 percent increase in high-scorers on Equanimity, contrasted with no change among students who study less than six hours per week. Apparently, being able to engage in sustained intellectual activity of this sort contributes to the development of the student's sense of equanimity. However, here we may have a situation where the causation is coming from the opposite direction; that is, students are better able to put in more time studying if they have experienced significant growth in equanimity during college. And, of course, the causation may be operating simultaneously in both directions. Resolving this ambiguity appears to require further research.

College faculty members can also contribute to the development of their students' sense of equanimity. Specifically, our data show that students' equanimity can be strengthened by attending a college where the faculty place a relatively strong emphasis on their own spirituality. The data suggest further that such faculty are especially likely to encourage students to express their own spirituality and to explore questions of meaning and purpose.

IMPEDIMENTS TO EQUANIMITY

Our data indicate that growth in equanimity during college can be negatively influenced by two factors: playing video or computer games and majoring in engineering. As it turns out, most of our measures of spiritual development show negative relationships with these two variables. In the case of engineering, at least two factors are worth considering: the heavy academic workload that most engineering majors are confronted with, and the nature of the peer group in the engineering field. Given the academic pressures that the typical engineering student experiences, it may well be difficult to find much time either for reflection or for the sorts of group activities that contribute to growth in equanimity. At the same time, since engineering students already score relatively low on Equanimity when they start college, each new class of engi-neering majors constitutes a peer group in which equanimity is not likely to be either modeled or encouraged.

Students who never play video or computer games—a little over half of our sample—show a gain of 6 percent in high-scorers on Equanimity, compared to a 1 percent gain among those who spend at least some time playing such games. While we can only speculate about the reasons for this negative effect, it seems clear that such games are typically characterized by a number of features—competitiveness, violence, tension—that would seem to be anathema to the cultivation of equanimity.

SUMMARY

Equanimity plays an important role in the quality of undergradu-ate students' lives because it shapes how they respond to their experiences, especially experiences that are potentially stressful. Our findings show that equanimity grows during the college years, and that practices such as meditation and self-reflection can con-tribute to that growth.

The current generation of students can look forward to an increasingly complex world, which inevitably will carry an inde-terminate amount of stress and strain. For these students, one thing is certain: the quality of their lives and whatever contribu-tions they may make to the world will ultimately be determined by their capacity to make meaning in the face of ambiguity, uncer-tainty, and change, particularly in the face of dislocating chal-lenges. How does meaning-making equip someone to deal with stress while avoiding automatic impulses, such as the fight-or-flight syndrome? We have already suggested that in our adult exemplars there is strong evidence of a meaning-making capacity which includes pause and reframing. Taking pause is extremely useful in that it permits one to dwell with a challenge or problem rather than going with a first impulse, which typically assumes the defensive posture of either lashing out (fighting) or running from (taking flight). The Dalai Lama has been determined to consider and find solutions to the situation of the Tibetan diaspora rather than react to it personally—even though the occupation has, at times, been posed in the most personal terms by the Chinese authorities. We know from the Dalai Lama's own account (1991) that the process he went through was one of pause and reframing, that is, transcending his immediate reaction (which was personal and visceral) and rechanneling the energy into reframing the problem in terms that take into account the partisan perceptions of his opponents. A similar process seems to be at work in the lives of most of our other exemplars.

We believe that the construct of Equanimity can be further understood by situating it in the larger context of stages of consciousness as set forth in the developmental schemes of theorists such as Fowler (1981), Gilligan (1982), Kegan (1982), Kohlberg (1981), Parks (2000), and Wilber (1996). Such "stage" theorists generally agree that the highest stages of consciousness are "transpersonal" in nature—that there exist stages where one begins to identify with a larger ("world-centric") impersonal reality. At these higher stages, as one gradually ceases to identify with a "separate self," responses to life challenges naturally begin to take into account the "greater good," in contrast to the ego-centric and ethnocentric perspectives that characterize one's typical response to stress, which we expect to encounter at lower stages of consciousness. Clearly, such transpersonal perspectives are conducive to the use of pause and reframing that we have postulated as fundamental to equanimity.

Our data suggest a number of very practical strategies that colleges and universities can employ to promote the development of equanimity among their undergraduate students: greater use of reflective, meditative, and contemplative practices both in and out of the classroom, and participation in group activities that are designed to serve others—community service, leadership training, and participation in student clubs and groups. We'll address these strategies at greater length in Chapter Nine when we explore the implications of this study for higher education.

CHAPTER FIVE

SPIRITUALITY IN PRACTICE
Caring For and About Others

Three of our measures of spirituality reflect the student's sense of caring about and connectedness to others: Ethic of Caring, Ecumenical Worldview, and Charitable Involvement. These three measures are all positively correlated with each other,[1] and each emphasizes a particular aspect of caring or connectedness: caring *about* others (Ethic of Caring), caring *for* others (Charitable Involvement), and a sense of connectedness to all beings (Ecumenical Worldview).

In Chapter One we described spirituality as involving our inner, subjective life. It is reflected in the values and beliefs we hold and in our sense of who we are, where we come from, and why we are here—the meaning we see in our lives. Spirituality is also about our sense of connectedness to one another and to the world around us. This sense of interconnectedness is very much present in definitions offered by other scholars. For example, the feminist scholar bell hooks (2000) conceptualized spirituality in terms of interconnectedness, transcendence, and one's engagement in teaching love. In her words, "spiritual life is first and foremost about commitment to a way of thinking and behaving that honors principles of inter-being and interconnectedness." This sense of interconnectedness clearly addresses the notion of interdependence, suggesting that "what we do to others, we do to ourselves." Caring for and about others is therefore very much an expression of one's spirituality. As one of our student interviewees said, "I feel most spiritually alive when I am working with the community and I am learning about their issues and how I can help them, and trying to be in solidarity with them."

In many ways, caring for and about the "other" bridges the notion of spirituality with many religious traditions that consider love and caring as critical to their faith's practice. For example, "Love thy neighbor as thyself" is a central principle in the Christian faith tradition. And "Seek to be in harmony with all your neighbors; live in amity with your brethren" is a tenet of Confucianism. To be "full of love for all things in the world, practicing virtue in order to benefit others; this person alone is happy" is a key point of Buddhism. As one of the faculty members we interviewed who identified herself as a Buddhist said, "one of the central teachings of Buddhism is compassion." A notion of caring for and about others is thus a common thread running through many of the world's established faith traditions.

It would seem that charitable involvement and an ethic of caring can grow from an ecumenical worldview—a feeling of oneness with the universe; seeing oneself as part of the weave, the fabric, of all life; an individual's sense of self in full integration with all of humanity. Caring and ecumenism also involve a sense of responsibility for the welfare of others, a transcendence of self that seeks to live in interpersonal communion. And charitable involvement is how we express our sense of caring and ecumenism, that is, in being socially responsible by virtue of feeling ourselves to be part of the cosmos and therefore our brothers' and sisters' keepers.

ETHIC OF CARING

The Ethic of Caring measure is composed of eight items that reflect our sense of caring and concern about the welfare of others and the world around us. These caring feelings for others are expressed in wanting to help those who may be troubled ("helping others who are in difficulty") and those who are suffering ("reducing pain and suffering in the world"). The feelings convey a concern about issues of social justice ("helping to promote racial understanding" and "trying to change things that are unfair in the world") and an interest in the welfare of one's community and the environment ("becoming involved in programs to clean up the environment" and "becoming a community leader"). They also serve as a foundation for wanting to engage in political activism ("influencing the political structure" and "influencing social values").

Nell Noddings, a renowned educator and scholar recognized for her work on the ethic of care, has spoken eloquently and persuasively of the importance of caring and the critical role education plays in developing in students such an ethic (Noddings, 1984, 1992, 2002). She believes that caring *about* others is the foundation for our sense of justice, which in turn leads to caring *for* others. Caring about, she explains, can be empty if it does not culminate in caring for.

It was reassuring to find that this quality of caring, as reflected in our empirically derived measure Ethic of Caring, grows during the college years. In fact, it is the spiritual quality that shows the greatest change, almost doubling in high-scorers between the freshman and junior years: 14 percent of entering college students scored high on Ethic of Caring; by the time they were completing their junior year, 27 percent received high scores on this measure.

Several of the items in the Ethic of Caring scale show a growth of 10 or more percentage points between 2004 and 2007: "helping others who are in difficulty" increases from 27 percent during the freshman year to reach 38 percent by end of the junior year; "reducing pain and suffering in the world" climbs from 55 to 67 percent; "becoming involved in programs to clean up the environment" rises from 17 to 30 percent; and "influencing social values" grows from 35 to 48 percent. Two of these items—"helping others who are in difficulty" and "reducing pain and suffering in the world"—represent activities that are driven by an empathetic understanding and a strong connection the self feels for the other. The other two items that show considerable growth over time—"becoming involved in programs to clean up the environment" and "influencing social values"—are concerns embedded in a strong sense of social responsibility.

While women compared to men score higher on Ethic of Caring during their first and third years in college, the overall growth in high-scorers that takes place during college is about the same for women and men: 13 and 12 percentage points, respectively. Examining changes by the type of college students attend, we find change and growth to be about the same for students across most types of institutions, the exceptions being students attending Evangelical institutions, who show even greater increases, growing from 17 percent of students who scored high as freshmen to 33 percent by the time they were completing their junior year; and students in secular institutions, who show the least growth, from 21 to 30 percent.

Different experiences that students encounter in secular versus Evangelical institutions can explain, at least in part, why the magnitude of change may vary. There are differences in religious identity, for example, between students who attend secular institutions as compared to Evangelical institutions, where well over half of the students identify themselves as Evangelical Christians. Also, there are often differences in curricular emphasis and in overall institutional culture. For example, one would expect a greater emphasis on Christian beliefs and practices at an Evangelical institution as compared to a secular one. Likewise, one would expect to find differences in course offerings dealing with the tenets of Christian faith, as in Christology. Thus, we must examine the overall institutional culture and the curriculum in each type of institution when we try to explain changes in values that are expressed through the spiritual measures we have identified.

In addition to variations in change and growth of Ethic of Caring that are based on gender or where students attend college, we also observe differences among students with different religious preferences. Upon entry into college, Hindu students and members of the Church of Christ express the strongest Ethic of Caring (44% and 35% high-scorers, respectively). By the end of their junior year they continue to be among the groups having the most high scores on Ethic of Caring (49% and 41% high-scorers, respectively) and are joined by Unitarian/Universalists (42%), Buddhists (49%), and Islamic students (47%). These three groups show more growth in Ethic of Caring during college (17 to 20 percentage point gain in high scores) than any of the other religious groups. Religious groups with the fewest high-scorers on Ethic of Caring at the end of the junior year include

Seventh-Day Adventists (12%), Quakers (14%), and Lutherans (17%).

ECUMENICAL WORLDVIEW

Although the eight-item measure of Ethic of Caring addresses "caring" in the sense of a personal commitment to alleviate the suffering of others, the twelve-item Ecumenical Worldview scale is primarily focused on seeing the world as an interconnected whole and on feeling a personal connection with, and acceptance of, all other beings. Eight of the twelve items directly reflect this sense of connectedness and acceptance: "feeling a strong connection to all humanity"; "believing in the goodness of all people"; believing that "all life is interconnected," and not only "having an interest in different religious traditions" but also believing that "love is at the root of all the great religions"; that "we are all spiritual beings"; that "non-religious people can lead lives that are just as moral as those of religious believers"; and that "most people can grow spiritually without being religious."

At the same time, Ecumenical Worldview also includes three items reflecting a personal commitment to act on this world-centric vision: "improving the human condition"; "improving my understanding of other countries and cultures"; and "accepting others as they are." Finally, and not surprisingly, students with a strong ecumenical worldview are also inclined to rate themselves highly on the trait "understanding of others." As one of our student interviewees reflected: "You cannot discount anyone else's religion, because they [may] find peace, even if it's a different form of God in their religion. And you have to respect that."

As with Ethic of Caring, there is growth as well in students' Ecumenical Worldview between the freshman and junior years: from 13 percent of students who score high on this quality when they start college, to 18 percent by the end of the junior year. The individual item that shows the greatest change relates to improving students' "understanding of other countries and cultures." It changes from 42 percent who indicated it was a "very important" or "essential" objective as freshmen, to 54 percent who considered it so as juniors. As we are becoming an increasingly global society, one would hope, indeed expect, that college attendance would have such an impact on student values as students are exposed to new ideas and knowledge, and as they encounter peers who are different from themselves. If we are to live as one world, interdependent economically, if we are to preserve our environment worldwide, and if we are ever going to find ways to transcend our racial, religious, ethnic, and national differences, then expanding our knowledge and understanding of other countries and cultures becomes essential.

As with Ethic of Caring, women score somewhat higher than men on the quality of Ecumenical Worldview during both their freshman and junior years. However, changes between the first and third years in college are similar across all types of colleges and universities. Entering college students who indicate their religious preferences as Unitarian, Quaker, or Hindu are the highest scorers on Ecumenical Worldview (26%–33% earn high scores). These groups continue to demonstrate high levels of Ecumenical Worldview as college juniors (38%–46% high-scorers) and are joined by Buddhists (36%). The three groups of juniors with the fewest high-scorers on Ecumenical Worldview (7%–9%) include Seventh-Day Adventists, Jews, and members of the Church of Christ.

When we compare these results with the results reported earlier for Ethic of Caring, we find three religious groups that tend to score high on *both* Ecumenical Worldview and Ethic of Caring: Buddhists, Hindus, and Unitarian/Universalists. What is it about these nonmainstream religious faith traditions that corresponds to an enhanced focus on connectedness and caring qualities? Is there something unique about their belief systems— perhaps a greater focus on compassion for others? Two things these faith traditions appear to have in common are openness to beliefs about deity, and a strong adherence to universal love and interconnectedness. For example, one of the shared beliefs of most Unitarian/Universalists is "respect for the interdependent web of all existence of which we are a part" ("Unitarian Universalist Association of Congregations," n.d.). This notion of the interconnectedness of all peoples is a central theme in all three traditions.

Another possibility is that students adhering to these faith traditions have had cultural experiences that differ from those of students in more mainstream faiths. In a recent article that explores the characteristics of students from nonmainstream religious traditions, Bryant (2006) reports that Buddhist and Hindu students are most likely to claim their racial identity as nonwhite. According to Bryant, 65 percent of Buddhists and 84 percent of Hindus indicate their identities as Asian American. Their experience of growing up in households that are likely to represent nonwhite cultural traditions may contribute to their being more ecumenical in their worldviews. Bryant also reports that more than 60 percent of religious-minority students rate themselves high on compassion, which may explain their high scores on the caring measures. At the same time, one of the basic principles espoused by Unitarian/Universalists is "justice, equity, and compassion in human relations" ("Unitarian Universalist Association of Congregations," n.d.).

CHARITABLE INVOLVEMENT

The third caring and connectedness measure, Charitable Involvement, is the behavioral counterpart to Ethic of Caring. It is composed of seven items, four of which involve some form of volunteer or community service work: "participated in community food or clothing drives," "performed community service as part of a class," "performed volunteer work," and hours spent in "volunteer work." The other items include "helped friends with personal problems," "donated money to charity," and a commitment to "participating in a community action program."

Charitable Involvement is the only spirituality measure that shows a net decline during the college years, from 12 percent of students receiving high scores as entering freshmen to 9 percent by the end of the junior year. However, when we examine the individual items in the scale we find that certain values and activities are in a distinct decline while others increase markedly. For example, *all* community service activities—doing volunteer work, performing service as part of a class, participating in food and clothing drives—decline in frequency between the freshman and junior years. The percentage doing any kind of volunteer work, for example, declines from 82 to 74 percent. Considering that such activities typically require a significant amount of time, such a decline is perhaps to be expected in light of the demands on one's time that most new college students experience. College students today find themselves very pressed for time under the greater demands of academic work in college combined with the need for many students to work in order to pay for their college expenses. (A similar argument may help to explain the decline in the Religious Engagement measure reported in the next chapter.)

Yet behaviors such as donating money to charity and helping friends with personal problems actually increase in frequency during college, as does the strength of students' commitment to participate in community action programs (the percentage who say that this is an "essential" or "very important" goal rises from 25% to 34%). As aptly said by a female student attending a large public research university, "I don't want to just do things for me. I want to do things for other people, and I really want to help out other people. And I think just helping other people and helping them become happy will make me happy."

We see substantial differences between women and men with respect to Charitable Involvement that replicate what we found with Ethic of Caring and Ecumenical Worldview: twice as many women as men score high on Charitable Involvement both as freshmen (15% vs. 7% receive high scores) and as juniors (12% vs. 6%). Moreover, while the patterns of growth or decline on the individual items are similar for women and men, on every item of the scale women score higher than do men. The observed declines over time in specific items are also somewhat less substantial for women.

Charitable involvement as a behavioral spiritual quality is highest among freshmen enrolling at Roman Catholic institutions, where 17 percent earn high scores, but students at Catholic colleges also show the largest decline during college (to 12%). Declines occur among students at all other types of institutions except those enrolled at Evangelical campuses, where there is actually a small increase (from 13% to 14%).

There are also some interesting religious differences with respect to Charitable Involvement. When they enter college as freshmen, Hindu, Buddhist, Islamic, and Eastern Orthodox students show the highest levels of Charitable Involvement (22%–32%). By their junior year, however, Buddhists and Eastern

Orthodox students show dramatic declines in Charitable Involvement, while Hindus show substantial increases, with 44 percent of Hindu juniors earning high scores. The only other religious group showing a substantial increase in Charitable Involvement during college is the Quakers, with the percentage of high-scorers nearly doubling from 13 to 25 percent. These increases among Hindus and Quakers are remarkable, given that overall we see a decline in Charitable Involvement across the total sample of students. The fact that Quakers and Hindus show large increases could be explained in part as a function of the cultures of these two faith traditions. Quakers are known for the importance they place on service as defined by and practiced through the American Friends Service Committee, a well-known charitable organization. At the same time, Hindus' strong awareness of and sensitivities toward poverty may result in their placing great importance on helping through acts of charity.

In sum, two of our measures of connectedness and caring—Ecumenical Worldview and Ethic of Caring—show substantial growth in high-scorers (from 13% to 18% and from 14% to 27%, respectively) between the freshman and junior years, whereas Charitable Involvement, a measure that depends heavily on students' available time, shows a modest decline from 12 to 9 percent. As mentioned earlier, this decline could be explained by students having less time for service activities, which results from the increased academic demands of college and, for many students, the time spent working to pay college expenses. In the near future we may well see an increase in students' Charitable Involvement, as more institutions create service-learning courses and expand opportunities for students to engage in volunteerism.

The ethic of service is becoming a more central value in both religious and secular institutions. One recent example is a large research university's designating a "day of service" for its entering class of over four thousand students, all of whom will participate in a volunteer service day in the surrounding community.

The fact that women score higher than men on all three measures of caring and connectedness is not surprising in light of prior research showing that women tend to be more relational and to exhibit higher levels of caring. Carol Gilligan, a former student and colleague of noted scholar Lawrence Kohlberg, who wrote extensively on students' moral development, challenged Kohlberg's previous work on the stages of moral development in part because it was based on research involving men only. Drawing on her research with women, Gilligan (1982) identified caring as a high stage of moral development, on par with Kohlberg's high stage of Fairness. Moreover, Josselson (1987) reports that identity development for women depends on relationships rather than transactions, and Belenky and colleagues (1986) emphasized the importance of connectedness in intellectual development as well as identity development for women. All of these authors and many others who have been interested in women's development have identified the importance of relationships in women's lives. Since women exhibit, cultivate, and are validated for such interests, it is no wonder that in all of our spiritual measures of caring and relatedness, women surpass men.

EFFECT OF COLLEGE EXPERIENCES

To learn how the college experience influences the development of an ethic of caring, an ecumenical worldview, and charitable involvement, we undertook separate analyses for each corresponding measure. As with the spiritual measures described in the two preceding chapters, in each analysis we first tried to take into account the student's initial level of the relevant quality (such as Ethic of Caring) as she was about to start college. We also took into account many other personal characteristics, including race, gender, and religious preference as well as prior experiences and behaviors (leadership experiences, community service, working experience, and so forth). By controlling for such entering characteristics, we hoped to gain a more valid picture of how the college experience influences the three caring and connectedness qualities (see the Appendix for more detail on methodology).

From there we focused on the nature and type of college experiences that could play a role in the development of each of the three spiritual qualities in the student. Specifically, we looked at the possible effects of the students' academic major, where they lived (on campus or at home) while attending college, and the type of institution they were attending. We also examined the possible effects on caring and connectedness of a number of other factors: relevant faculty characteristics, such as the faculty's own level of spirituality and their attitudes about the role of spirituality in education and the nature of faculty-student interactions; characteristics of students' peers; and students' academic and cocurricular experiences. We also wanted to determine whether engagement in personal activities such as meditation, prayer, and readings on religious matters plays a role in how students grow and change with respect to these three spiritual measures (see Appendix for variables used in the analysis).

MAJORS

Not surprisingly, certain majors have a clear effect on how students change with respect to the three caring and connectedness measures. Students majoring in either the social sciences or the biological sciences show larger-than-average increases between their freshman and junior years on Ethic of Caring and Charitable Involvement. Majoring in history/political science is also associated with larger increases in Ethic of Caring. By contrast, students majoring in engineering, math, or statistics are more likely to show decreases over time on both of these measures as well as on Ecumenical Worldview. Business majors also tend to show declines in Ecumenical Worldview. It thus appears that the more person-oriented fields—social science, history and political science, and subfields of the biological sciences—lead students to feel more connected with and caring about others, while fields that are more impersonal and abstract—engineering, business, math, and statistics—have the opposite effect. Perhaps the epistemology of these latter fields, coupled with certain prevalent beliefs ("If you cannot measure it, it does not exist") shared by many who teach and study in the fields, is antithetical to notions of an inner life that needs to be attended to and nurtured in order to develop a sense of caring or connectedness with other people. These findings could also be attributable to a peer group effect, since students who choose majors in mathematics, engineering, or business as entering freshmen are already scoring low on these three measures when they begin college. Whatever the explanation, these findings suggest that if institutions wish to cultivate engineering, math, and business students' sense of caring and connectedness to others, they might examine the dominant values and assumptions that characterize students and faculty in these fields. Such an examination might suggest strategies for encouraging these students to give greater priority to developing their sense of caring and connectedness to others.

FACULTY

Our data show that college faculty can have a significant impact on students' sense of caring and connectedness. For example, interacting with faculty outside of class is positively associated with growth in all three measures of student caring and connectedness. Further, faculty who are highly "student-centered" in their teaching methods are much more likely than other faculty to facilitate student growth in an ethic of caring and in charitable involvement. Student-centered teaching methods take a more individualized and interactive approach to instruction, in contrast to traditional teaching methods, in which the teacher is the "knower" and the student is the vessel where the teacher's knowledge is deposited. One way of looking at student-centered teaching is that it demonstrates the faculty's own ethic of caring about their students, a sense of caring that is modeled in how students are taught and evaluated. Faculty who are student-centered in their pedagogy are much more likely to use cooperative learning, engage students in group projects, encourage them to evaluate each other's work, and ask students to recommend and select topics for the course (Lindholm and Astin, 2008).

Clearly, faculty who relate in such ways to their students are not only acting as caring role models but also utilizing practices that help students become more self-aware and grow in self-efficacy. Giving students responsibility for selecting topics of study or evaluating each other's work is self-empowering. Moreover, participating in group projects, engaging in cooperative learning, and evaluating each other's work all help students develop an understanding of others and a sense of responsibility and caring.

Elsewhere we have reported that faculty members who consider themselves to be spiritual in their orientation are more likely to be student-centered in their pedagogy (Lindholm and Astin,

2008). We believe that faculty who are in touch with their own spirituality and who see the importance of spirituality in their own lives are likely to exhibit certain behaviors, both in and outside the classroom, that support the development of caring in their students. Such faculty members are also more likely to engage in conversations with students about values, and about the meaning and purpose of life, all of which can affect students' spiritual growth and development. As one female faculty member told us in response to the question, "How do you know that you touch the lives of students?": "Well, one tangible way I can tell is how they respond to me. If I can touch the life of one person beyond the 'book,' then I have made a difference in the course I teach. I consider my purpose in the class beyond the 'books.' I bring in values. Not imposing mine, but I do talk about values. It may be one day about their work habits. It may be about 'why they are doing sloppy work.'"

One of our most important findings concerns faculty who encourage and involve students in conversations about matters of meaning and purpose in life; who engage them in discussions of religion and spirituality; and who may also act as spiritual role models by virtue of their own spiritual beliefs and practices. Our findings provide strong evidence that such faculty play a critical role in facilitating students' sense of caring and feelings of connectedness with others.

As we mentioned earlier, between the freshman and junior years there is an overall growth of 13 percent in the number of students who score high on Ethic of Caring. However, when we examine students separately in how much their faculty encouraged them to "explore questions of meaning and purpose," we find substantial differences: among students whose faculty frequently encouraged them to explore such questions, there was a 19 percent increase in the number of high-scorers on Ethic of Caring; among students whose faculty never encouraged such exploration, there was only an 8 percent increase. (Students whose faculty occasionally encouraged them to explore such questions fell in between, with a 12 percent increase.)

Faculty encouragement to explore questions of meaning and purpose had an even more dramatic effect on students' Ecumenical Worldview scores. Figure 5.1 separates the students into three

FIGURE 5.1. FREQUENCY OF "BEING ENCOURAGED TO EXPLORE QUESTIONS OF MEANING AND PURPOSE" AND ECUMENICAL WORLDVIEW

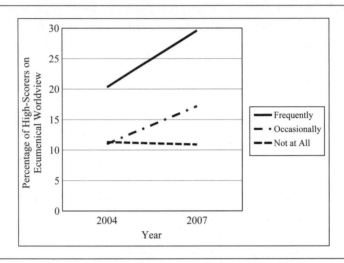

groups according to the frequency of faculty encouragement to engage in such exploration. Students whose faculty never encourage them to explore questions of meaning and purpose (the bottom line in the figure) show no increase in high-scorers between 2004 and 2007, while those whose faculty frequently give such encouragement (top line) show a substantial increase of 10 percent in high-scorers on Ecumenical Worldview. Students who receive occasional encouragement (middle line) show a 6 percent increase. Of particular significance is that the "occasionally" and "not at all" groups had significantly different percentages of high-scorers on Ecumenical Worldview in 2007 (junior year), even though their 2004 (freshman) percentages were virtually identical.

Such analyses not only highlight the relationship between faculty encouragement and student change but also shed some light on the question of whether the changes we are observing are simply a function of maturation rather than being attributable to the effects of the college experience. If the growth in an ethic of caring or ecumenical worldview were merely maturational, or what might be considered a normal trajectory for psychological development among young adults at this stage in life, the amount of change would not vary according to what experiences the students had during college. The fact that all three groups of students show some growth in an ethic of caring might suggest a maturational process, but the fact that the *amount* of growth varies systematically according to how much encouragement students receive from professors suggests that at least some of the observed growth is attributable to the college experience. In the case of Ecumenical Worldview, the fact that the "no encouragement" group showed *no* change in the percentage of high-scorers provides even more support for the notion that the college experience, and not just maturation, accounts in part for the growth in this quality during the college years.

Certain practices that a few faculty use in the classroom can also bear an important relationship to how students grow and change in their caring and sense of connectedness. For example, our data suggest that faculty can have a substantial impact on students' spiritual development through the use of contemplation or meditation in the classroom. Although only one student in five reports that any of his or her faculty employ contemplation or meditation in their classes, we find that these students show significantly larger score gains on both Ethic of Caring and Ecumenical Worldview than do students whose faculty never use such techniques. Further, these same students who report that some of their professors have employed contemplation or meditation in class show no decline in Charitable Involvement, unlike the overall student sample.

Evidence is accumulating on the impact of such practices on learning and other educational outcomes as well. In a forthcoming article in the *Teachers College Record* based on a review of meditative practices in higher education, Shauna Shapiro and colleagues (forthcoming) report that meditation enhances cognitive and academic performance, assists in the management of academic-related stress, and contributes to the development of the "whole person." Along with other classroom practices, such as reflective writing and journaling, meditation was found to be a powerful mechanism for encouraging students to focus inwardly, to contemplate issues of purpose and meaning, and to gain greater self-awareness. The use of reflection in service learning has been found to enable students to develop a greater awareness, not only about themselves but also about the "other," that is, those they serve (Jacoby and Associates, 1996; Rhoads and Howard, 1998; Sax and Astin, 1997).

Encouraging students to be reflective and to journal in class exposes them to the power of these techniques and related processes in their everyday life. It is not surprising that when students engage in such activities outside the classroom, they accrue benefits in feeling more interconnected with others, and in caring about and for others.

Our data reveal still another aspect of faculty beliefs and behaviors that can play a role in facilitating students' sense of caring and connectedness, namely, the importance faculty place on having a diverse campus population. This faculty measure reflects beliefs such as the following: that their institution should emphasize diversity more strongly in its curriculum; that a racially and ethnically diverse student body enhances the educational experience; and that enhancing the student's knowledge and appreciation of other racial and ethnic groups is a critical goal for undergraduate education. Faculty who hold such beliefs tend to facilitate growth in students' ecumenical worldview, a spiritual quality that is defined in part by values such as "having an interest in different religious traditions," "feeling a strong connection to all humanity," and commitment to "improving my understanding of other countries and cultures."

For the last four decades many of us have participated in efforts to bring about a greater degree of equity and fairness in education and at work. Starting with the civil rights movement, the women's movement, and more recently the gay rights movement, society as a whole has gradually come to recognize that we are all one, and that differential treatment of others based on their racial or ethnic identity, gender, or sexual orientation is inherently unjust and immoral. In order to become more inclusive, we also have to believe in the basic goodness of each person and in our interdependence. So it is no wonder that those faculty who have done the personal work of cultivating their own sense of love and caring for the other would also believe in the power of inclusivity and its importance in the student body and in the curriculum. An institutional social justice agenda goes hand in hand with the development of one's spirituality as reflected in qualities such as an ethic of caring, an ecumenical worldview, and charitable involvement. We concur with the meaning of "social justice" provided by Jacqueline Powers Doud, president of Mount St. Mary's College: "Social justice relates to the obligation on everyone's part to improve social structures and institutions so that they work more effectively on behalf of the common good."

LIVING ARRANGEMENTS

Residential campuses, where students live on campus rather than commute, also play an important role in developing students' ethic of caring, ecumenical worldview, and charitable involvement. The fact that living on campus exposes students to others with diverse religious beliefs and cultural backgrounds no doubt helps to explain this effect. Being exposed to, and learning about, "otherness" is a key to becoming other-directed in that it expands one's horizons, helping to shift the orientation of one's consciousness from an ethnocentric or egocentric perspective to a world-centric or transpersonal perspective. This interpretation is further reinforced by findings, reported next, regarding the impact of curricular and cocurricular experiences.

CURRICULAR, COCURRICULAR, AND PERSONAL EXPERIENCES

A number of distinct campus experiences directly affect growth in students' ethic of caring, ecumenical worldview, and charitable involvement. Some of the strongest effects are associated with self-reflection, a practice that leads to larger-than-average increases in students' ethic of caring and ecumenical worldview; and meditation, which appears to facilitate growth on all three "connectedness" measures. Since both meditation and self-reflection were also shown to enhance growth in the other two spiritual measures (Spiritual Quest and Equanimity; see Chapters Three and Four), these results provide further evidence in support of the notion that "inner work" is critical to spiritual development.

At this point we should mention that other than majoring in engineering or math, only one student activity appears to impede growth in all three measures of caring and connectedness: watching television. In many respects the act of watching television, in which one's attention is entirely focused on external sounds and images, is anathema to the mindfulness and self-awareness that is involved in meditation and reflection.

Another important set of findings concerns the individual experiences that make up the Charitable Involvement measure: volunteer work, helping friends with personal problems, donating money to charity, and participating in community service as part of an academic course. Each of these four experiences appears to enhance growth in the other two "connectedness" measures, Ethic of Caring and Ecumenical Worldview. Personal involvement in charitable activities, in short, enhances students' sense of caring and connectedness to others.

Several other academic and cocurricular experiences show significant positive relationships to growth in caring and connectedness: studying abroad, taking interdisciplinary courses, discussing religion with others, hours per week spent studying, and reading religious/spiritual material other than sacred texts.

Studying abroad, discussing religion, and community service enlarge students' perspectives in countless ways by exposing them to a diversity of peoples, ideas, and cultures. Among many other things, such experiences allow students to reflect on what they have in common with others. While encountering such differences helps students to examine preconceived notions and beliefs about self and other, it also lets them recognize their oneness with others and the world. Likewise, interdisciplinary courses give students an opportunity to see how different areas of study and different epistemologies explain various phenomena. Seeing such diversity in intellectual perspectives and interpretations may also lead to an appreciation, and an enhanced understanding, of the importance of respecting differing points of view. Most of these curricular experiences—especially studying abroad, taking interdisciplinary courses, and engaging in community service as part of a class—can develop critical thinking by moving students from a dualistic knowing (authorities know; there is only one "right" perspective) to relativism (everything is relative to something else; you have to understand how each context works). Exposing students to interdisciplinary studies thus enhances their cognitive development as well as their ethical development. In the words of Perry (1981), who developed this schema of cognitive and ethical growth, "this is how life is, in that students recognizing this truth will fight for their own values while respecting the values of others."

Our analyses also show that students who socialize with people from other races grow in feeling overall more interconnected and caring. This finding not only underscores the importance of creating opportunities for students to encounter and interact with others who are different from them but also provides more supporting evidence for those who have been advocating for greater racial diversity in college admissions (Orfield, 2001).

The value of interacting with diverse student peers is further reinforced by several other findings suggesting that cocurricular experiences can also promote students' sense of caring and connectedness if they put students in close contact with one another and allow them to collaborate. For example, we find that students who are more actively engaged in campus clubs and organizations, or who belong to religious organizations, are more likely to grow and develop in an ethic of caring, ecumenical worldview, and charitable involvement. This also holds true for those who are members of sororities and fraternities, and for those who participate in student government and leadership training. All of these experiences speak to the exposure of students to group activities and to interactions with others rather than choosing to live a more solitary life.

SUMMARY

Two of our measures of caring and connectedness—Ethic of Caring and Ecumenical Worldview—show significant growth during the college years, while the third measure, Charitable Involvement, declines between the freshman and junior years. Since two kinds of charitable activities—donating money to charity and helping friends with personal problems—actually increase in frequency after the student enters college, the overall decline in Charitable Involvement scores appears to be entirely attributable to the decline in various forms of community service participation.

Students tend to show the greatest degree of growth on these three measures if they are actively engaged in self-reflection, contemplation, or meditation. Engaging in this same "inner work" was also found to contribute to the development of our other two spiritual measures, Spiritual Quest (Chapter Three) and Equanimity (Chapter Four).

Women consistently score higher than men on all three measures of caring and connectedness, and Hindus, Buddhists, and Unitarian/Universalists obtain higher scores than students of other religious faiths. When it comes to the type of college the student attends, changes in these three measures over time are similar, except in the case of Evangelical colleges, where growth in Ethic of Caring is greater than average and where there is actually a slight increase in Charitable Involvement.

While exposure to social sciences or biological sciences strengthens the qualities represented by our Ethic of Caring, Ecumenical Worldview, and Charitable Involvement measures, majoring in technical fields such as engineering, math, statistics, or business has a negative impact on students' growth in these same qualities. The qualities of caring and relatedness are also enhanced by living on campus, participating in student government, discussing religion with others, and participating in clubs and organizations; all such experiences are likely to expose students to others who may hold diverse perspectives.

Another potentially powerful influence on students' sense of caring and connectedness is the faculty, especially faculty who encourage and involve students in conversations about matters of meaning and purpose in life; who value diversity; and who employ various forms of student-centered pedagogy. Caring and a sense of connectedness can also be promoted by curricular practices that enable students to engage with others who have different life experiences and perspectives, and that expose them to a diversity of intellectual approaches and perspectives—practices that include study abroad, service learning, and interdisciplinary studies.

CHAPTER SIX

THE RELIGIOUS LIFE
OF COLLEGE STUDENTS

Judging from their responses to the entering freshman survey, American college students are a pretty religious lot. Four out of five (80%) attended religious services during the year prior to entering college (44% attended frequently); more than three-fourths (77%) say they believe in God (another 16% are "not sure"); and more than two-thirds (69%) pray.

Religiousness generally involves devotion to, and practice of, some kind of faith tradition. It also typically involves membership in a community of fellow believers and participation in the rituals of the faith. Recall from Chapter Two that we developed three scales to measure how religious any student is: Religious Commitment, Religious Engagement, and Religious/Social Conservatism. These measures are intended to tell us three things regarding each student's degree of religiousness: how *committed* the student is to a religious faith, how *engaged* the student is in the practices of that faith, and how *conservative* the student's religious views and beliefs are.

Determining how religious development compares with spiritual development is of central interest in this study. Even though many people are inclined to think that religiousness and spirituality are pretty much the same thing, we are in a position here to see how similar they really are because we have developed separate measures of each. As we have done in earlier chapters with our measures of spirituality, in this chapter we will use our measures to look at how religiousness changes during the college years and how various college experiences contribute to these changes.

MEASURES OF RELIGIOUSNESS

Religious Commitment is an "internal" quality comprising twelve attitudinal and belief items. It reflects the student's self-rating on "religiousness" as well as the degree to which the student seeks to follow religious teachings in everyday life; finds religion to be personally helpful; and gains personal strength by trusting in a higher power. In particular, it measures the extent to which students' "spiritual/religious beliefs" play a central role in their life.

Religious Engagement, an "external" measure that represents the behavioral counterpart to Religious Commitment, includes nine items reflecting behaviors such as attending religious services, praying, religious singing/chanting, and reading sacred texts.

Religious/Social Conservatism is a seven-item measure reflecting the student's degree of opposition to such things as casual sex and abortion, how frequently the student prays for forgiveness, and the belief that people who don't believe in God will be punished. It also involves a commitment to proselytize and an inclination to see God as a father-figure. (One might also label this measure as "fundamentalism.")

These three measures are highly correlated, by which we mean that students who are strongly committed to a religious faith are also likely to engage in religious activities frequently and to score high on Religious/Social Conservatism.

In our analyses of students' spiritual development (Chapters Three, Four, and Five) we found that most spiritual qualities show positive growth during the college years. One of the key questions to be explored in the present chapter is whether religious development follows a similar pattern. What kinds of religious changes do students show during the college years?

CHANGES IN RELIGIOUS COMMITMENT

When they entered college as new freshmen, roughly two-thirds of the students endorsed each of the following statements from the Religious Commitment scale:

"I gain spiritual strength by trusting in a higher power."
"I find religion to be personally helpful."

"My spiritual/religious beliefs provide me with strength, support, and guidance."

"My spiritual/religious beliefs have helped me to develop my identity."

By the time the students had completed their junior year, these percentages had changed very little, suggesting that *students' level of Religious Commitment changes very little during college.* This conclusion is further supported by the fact that the number of students with high scores on Religious Commitment remained at 23 percent between 2004 and 2007.

This lack of growth in religious commitment during college is especially significant in light of the fact that most *spiritual* qualities appear to be enhanced by the college experience (see Chapters Three, Four, and Five). As we shall see shortly, the results with Religious Engagement and Religious/Social Conservatism actually show declines, reinforcing the conclusion that religiousness and spirituality diverge during the college years, despite the fact that they tend to be positively related.

So far we have been talking about the level of Religious Commitment of the entire student group. What about individual students? Fewer than 30 percent of the students change their freshman level of commitment (high, middle, or low) during college, and extreme changes are rare: only 1 percent of those who enter college scoring either high or low switch to the other extreme (from low to high, or from high to low). The scale item showing the largest change during the three years of college is the student's self-rating on "religiousness," where the number rating themselves "above average" or "top 10%" drops from 34 to 31 percent. In all likelihood this is a reflection of the significant decline in Religious Engagement (see below).

Despite the overall stability in students' level of religious commitment during college, some students will be inclined to raise or lower their level of commitment during the college years depending on how religiously *engaged* they are. The religious activity with by far the most powerful effect on Religious Commitment is prayer, followed by reading sacred texts and religious singing or chanting. Students who frequently engage in such activities after they enter college will be especially likely to raise their level of religious commitment while in college, while those who abstain from such activities are most likely to lower their commitment level. Therefore, religious commitment can be strengthened considerably by religious engagement (and, conversely, religious commitment will tend to decline if it is not accompanied by religious engagement).

This connection between engagement and commitment appears in several of our student interviews, as evidenced by this comment from a female student attending a historically black college in the South: "When I was younger, I was angry with God. I didn't want to go to church; I didn't want to do anything because I was mad at the cards that I was dealt in life. So, I was, like, 'Why do I have to go to church when we're poor, when my daddy's not around, when there's other things that other people have, and we're struggling? Why do I have to go to church when I have epilepsy?' And it was just a lot that I was really just angry about, you know? So, it was hard for me because it was only me, and my Mama. I'm the only child, and just coming here [to college] made me kind of [*holding back tears*] realize: okay, God has done all this for me, so I can't be mad at God anymore. So, going to Chapel, and being involved with [name of Chapel organization] and everything, it made me aware of all of the things that I've been blessed with. So, it was, like, 'Okay, now I'm going to try to have a relationship with God.'"

As it turns out, the relationship between prayer and changes in religious commitment during college is one of the strongest "experiential effects" found in the entire study. Thus, if we look only at the majority of students who start college with a medium level of Religious Commitment, more than one in four (27%) will shift to a high level of commitment if they pray on a daily basis while in college. Among those who start college with a medium level of commitment but don't pray while attending college, less than one in thirty (2.7%) will shift to a high level of commitment. At the same time, one in three (33%) of the students who don't pray while attending college will drop from a medium to a low level of commitment, compared to less than one in a hundred (0.9%) of those who pray daily. If you begin college then with a medium level of Religious Commitment, whether you raise or lower your level of commitment will have a lot to do with whether, and how much, you engage in prayer while attending college.

College activities that are found to strengthen students' level of Religious Commitment include engaging in volunteer work, donating money to charity, joining a campus religious organization, and discussing religion with peers, faculty, or staff. As one student attending a public university tells us, "I'm having discussions about spirituality or religion all the time. Well, since I've been at [this campus], you would not believe how many spiritual debates and conflicts I've been in."

The mechanism whereby membership in a campus religious organization strengthens religious commitment may be similar to that of religious singing: in both cases the student's beliefs would tend to be reinforced by participation in group activities involving others who share similar beliefs. The same may be true of discussing religion, since such discussions may well take place as part of a religious organization's activities. Volunteering and donating money to charity, of course, can be group activities that occur in connection with attendance at religious services, a key component of religious engagement (see below).

Although joining a campus religious organization and discussing religion with others are not part of the Religious Engagement scale, both activities could be considered as forms of religious engagement. It is not surprising that they, like the activities making up the Religious Engagement scale, tend to strengthen the student's religious commitment.

Two other activities that have a positive effect on religious commitment are self-reflection and meditation. That some students may be interpreting these two activities as being similar to, or part of, prayer is suggested by the fact that their effects on Religious Commitment are considerably diminished once we take into account the effect of prayer.

Some evidence also suggests that faculty can influence students' religious commitment if they encourage "discussion of religious/spiritual matters," or "personal expression of spirituality" in their students, or act as "spiritual role models." This kind of faculty encouragement appears to enhance religious commitment in part because it leads students to read sacred texts or other religious or spiritual literature, and it can also influence students directly by encouraging them to explore their faith in deeper terms. As one female faculty member at a Catholic university explains:

"The class that I taught was religion and the theories of Freud and Jung. I really liked working with students through Freud's and Jung's challenges to religion, which often helped the students clarify and articulate their own sense of who they were as religious or spiritual people. And I think it helped them have a broader sense of tolerating ambiguity. When I first started teaching, we often talked in that course about the political and economic dimensions of Christian beliefs and practices and theologies. And I sometimes did have students come into my office saying, 'Oh my God, you know what we've been talking about is how politics lead to theological statements and really having a kind of crisis of faith, because they thought it was straight from God. And Oh my God, people debating as human beings came up with these statements.' So there it was rather lovely to work with students toward an understanding that faith can accommodate doubt, and that theology can accommodate politics. And sometimes that was this world-shaking opening for students: 'Oh my, God can work through human beings. Who knew?'"

Three activities associated with declines in students' level of Religious Commitment are playing video games, alcohol consumption, and partying. While partying and alcohol consumption often go together, partying appears to be the more critical factor, since the effect of alcohol consumption disappears once the effect of partying is taken into account. Drinking per se does not appear to affect religious commitment. (Here we have another instance where the causation could be working in either direction; that is, while partying could serve to weaken religious commitment, it could also increase as a consequence of a decline in religious commitment.)

That some students are capable of simultaneously accommodating strong religious beliefs and partying is revealed in the following quote from a student: "Partying is something that's really, really hyped and really, really accessible in college more so than in other places, and so I know that the Bible speaks against that but I do understand that my partying is not taking me away from what I was taught. It's just more [that] this is all part of growing, this is all part of just going through college, matriculating or whatever, and I go through these experiences, but I'm not forgetting my background or my foundation. That was one of the things that I sort of grappled with at first, but now I think that I'm [coming] to accept it."

Religious Engagement

Attendance at religious services shows a steep decline during college. While a little more than half of the students (54%) attend services in college at about the same rate as they did in high school, more than a third (39%) attend less frequently, compared to only 7 percent who increase their frequency of attendance after entering college. As a result, the rate of frequent attendance declines from 44 percent in high school to 25 percent in college, and the rate of nonattendance nearly doubles (from 20% to 38%).

There are several possible reasons why students' level of Religious Engagement declines during the college years. One explanation is that many students leave home to attend college. Being away from direct parental influence for the first time could well increase the chances that the student will cease to attend religious services. Our data suggest that while leaving home appears to make some difference, it is by no means the sole explanation. Thus, among students who live on campus, nonattendance at religious services increases from 20 to 38 percent, but there is also a (somewhat smaller) increase in nonattendance among students who continue to live at home while attending college, from 20 to 32 percent. These data suggest a further explanation: simply attending college causes the student to spend less time with family and more time in the company of the diverse students who constitute most college peer groups. Such alterations in the students' environments could well increase the likelihood that they will abandon some of the customary behaviors that are part of family tradition. This sort of family and peer influence is illustrated in the following excerpt from one of our interviews with a male student at a Catholic college:

Q: Do you attend religious services?

A: Once in a while. And the reason I do is mostly because Mom's like, "Oh, do you want to go with me to church?" And I'm like, "Okay, yes." … Yes, whenever I go, I go with my mom, or I went with my girlfriend last year, too.

Q: But in general, you don't go by yourself?

A: No.

Q: So do you go for other people because they want you to go?

A: Basically, yes.

Q: You could say "No," but what's the reason you don't say "No"?

A: I guess probably just because it makes them happy, so I go.

Q: And you want to make them happy?

A: Yes. That or sometimes they'll nag me for a very long time [*laughs*].

The pressures of exams, study, and work may also lead college students to alter some of their previously established religious practices. Given that college students spend more time studying but still get lower grades than they did in high school (see Chapter Eight), it is not surprising that "something has to give." As one student told us in a personal interview: "Even though I ask these questions, or I talk to God on a regular basis, it's like there are still parts of me that I don't explore all the way because I say, 'Okay. Now I have to go study,' or 'I have to go do this,' you know, just to get my mind off of it. And, at the end of the day, I don't have time to dwell, and say, 'Hmmm.' You know?" Or as one of our focus group participants remarked, "I put less value in external factors like going to church and stuff, because it doesn't really seem that important to me to like lose sleep and go to church, because sleep is good for grades, and grades are good for what I'm going to do for the rest of my life."

This comment suggests that another possible explanation for the decline in attendance at religious services might relate to partying and drinking, both of which were found to have a negative effect on Religious Engagement, and both of which show substantial increases between high school and college. Compared to their last year in high school, twice as many college juniors drink beer frequently (26% vs. 13%) and consume wine or liquor frequently (23% vs. 11%), and larger numbers party for at least three hours per week (48% vs. 41%). (In contrast to what we found in the case of Religious Commitment, alcohol consumption continues to show a negative effect on Religious Engagement even after we take into account the effects of partying.) Could it be that drinking and partying cause more students to miss religious services because they are sleeping in late, or because they are hung over? We should also recognize, once again, that the causation might be working in the other direction, that is, that students might be less likely to consume alcohol *if* they continue to be active participants in their religious community while attending college.

During college this substantial decline in student attendance at religious services is accompanied by much smaller declines (2%–4%) in the rate of student participation in virtually all the other activities contained in the Religious Engagement scale: praying, religious singing/chanting, reading sacred texts, other readings on religion/spirituality, and attendance at classes, workshops, or retreats on matters related to religion/spirituality. As all of these activities can occur in connection with participation in a religious organization, it seems likely that these declines can be attributed, at least in part, to the lower frequency of student attendance at religious services.

These declines in religious engagement can be attenuated somewhat if the student engages in any of a number of activities, including joining a campus religious organization, taking religious studies classes, going on a religious mission trip, engaging in self-reflection or meditation, and discussing religion with peers, professors, or staff. Note that most of these activities also enhance religious commitment, which is perhaps to be expected, given that commitment and engagement are so strongly associated. Although donating money to charity and performing volunteer work are also associated with increased religious commitment during college, the causation here could, once more, be working the other way: students will be more likely to donate money to their religious organizations and to become involved in church-sponsored community service *if* they continue to attend services while they are attending college.

Religious engagement can also be affected by the student's major field of study. Majoring in any one of three fields—

agriculture, engineering, and the social sciences—is associated with a larger-than-average decline in Religious Engagement, while majoring in education is associated with a smaller-than-average decline. In the case of engineering and education, these may well be peer group effects, since most entering classes of engineering students include a disproportionate number who are religiously disengaged, while most entering classes of education students include a disproportionate number who are highly engaged. That these two fields would attract very different kinds of students is consistent with a large body of research (see, for example, Holland, 1985).

RELIGIOUS/SOCIAL CONSERVATISM

Religious/Social Conservatism reflects students' positions on issues such as abortion, casual sex, and atheism, as well as an inclination to proselytize and to see God as a father-figure. Like Religious Engagement, students' level of Religious/Social Conservatism declines during college. All but one of the seven items making up this scale show declines, with the largest drop— from 48 to 40 percent—occurring in the percentage of students who *dis*agree with the proposition that abortion should be legal, which shows that students are becoming more inclined to accept the "pro-choice" position on this controversial topic. Other sizable drops occur with two other items: "People who don't believe in God will be punished" (from 35% to 29% agreement), and "If two people really like each other, it's all right for them to have sex even if they've known each other for only a very short time" (from 55% to 48% *dis*agreement), suggesting a liberalization of attitudes concerning atheism and casual sex. The only item showing a conservative trend is the tendency to see God as a "father-figure," which grew from 37 to 41 percent of the students. Since all conceptions of God (creator, divine presence, nature, and so on) show increases during college in the percentage of students who endorse them, this finding may reflect the students' growing awareness of different theologies and different religious traditions.

In attempting to understand students' reduced conservatism, keep in mind that the "conservative" response to most of these items is a minority view among college students in general. In other words, many students who start college espousing highly conservative views on casual sex and abortion will be exposed to large numbers of new peers who may not necessarily share their beliefs on such issues, an experience that may lead some of them to question their beliefs. Moreover, evangelism may not be as well received in an environment where openness and acceptance of diversity in belief systems and practices are promoted. As one of the students in our focus groups observes, "So trying to figure out the truth and how do we worship together without offending one another ... that's one of the biggest issues that I have now."

Our data analysis shows that by far the strongest factor strengthening students' level of Religious/Social Conservatism during college is Religious Engagement. Students will be much less likely to show declines in Religious/Social Conservatism (and more likely to show increases) if they engage in any of the following religious activities: prayer, religious singing/chanting, reading sacred texts, and reading other religious/spiritual works. Each of these activities, of course, is part of the Religious Engagement scale. Other activities that promote religious/social conservatism include joining a campus religious organization, meditating, and going on a religious mission trip. Another weak but statistically significant positive effect on Religious/Social Conservatism is associated with participating in intercollegiate football or basketball. One possible explanation for this finding is that the "macho" image that one associates with such sports tends to promote conservative values on social issues. (Earlier studies of college students have shown that participation in intercollegiate football or basketball is associated with the development of conservative values, as well as greater tolerance of what has come to be known as "date rape." See Astin, 1993; Korn, 1996.) Given that many of these "revenue sports" teams (men's basketball and football) engage in group prayer before, during, and after games, and given the powerful peer group solidarity that is typically promoted by the coaches, it is perhaps not surprising to find such an effect.

That the student's degree of Religious/Social Conservatism can be influenced by peers is suggested by three variables that have positive effects on this measure: the *mean* Religious/Social

Conservatism of the peer group, participation in student clubs and groups, and participation in group projects. And, as is the case with Religious Commitment and Religious Engagement, Religious/Social Conservatism is positively associated with donating money to charity and negatively associated with partying and drinking.

ROLE OF DENOMINATIONAL PREFERENCE

Students vary a lot in their degree of religiousness, depending on what their religious preference is when they start college. The prominent role that religion plays in contemporary politics and society—political unrest in the Middle East, terrorism, the involvement of clergy in sexual transgressions, alliances between politicians and religious fundamentalists, to name a few—and the current attempts by many colleges and universities to promote greater communication and understanding among students of different religious persuasions, make it enlightening to understand how different denominations compare in their degree of religiousness.

Let's start with Religious Commitment. Although fewer than one entering freshman in four (23%) score high on Religious Commitment, much higher proportions of Baptists (46%), Mormons (55%), Muslims (38%), Seventh-Day Adventists (39%), and "other Christians" (44%) obtain high scores. Students with the lowest levels of commitment—all with less than 6 percent high-scorers—include Buddhists, Jews, Unitarian/Universalists, and students whose preference is "none."

We find a similar pattern with Religious Engagement, where only 20 percent of students in general obtain high scores. The most highly engaged students include Baptists (39%), Mormons (59%), Seventh-Day Adventists (50%), and other Christians (40%), while the least engaged are, once again, Buddhists (6%), Jews (7%), Unitarian/Universalists (4%), and students with no religious preference (1%).

When it comes to Religious/Social Conservatism, where only 16 percent of freshmen in general receive high scores, the most conservative groups are Baptists (38%), Mormons (36%), and other Christians, predominantly nondenominational (36%). The least conservative groups include Buddhists (0%), Hindus (1%), Jews (1%), Unitarian/Universalists (0%), and students with no religious preference (1%).

In short, it would appear that all three measures of religiousness generate highly similar patterns when it comes to students' religious preference, with the highest levels of commitment, engagement, and conservatism being shown by Baptists, Mormons, and other Christians, and the lowest levels occurring among Buddhists, Jews, Unitarian/Universalists, and students with no religious preference. One quality that clearly distinguishes these two groups is evangelism: Many if not most Baptists, Mormons, and other Christians share a strong tradition of evangelism, while most Buddhists, Jews, and Unitarian/Universalists do not.

Roman Catholic students show a unique pattern when it comes to religiousness, but especially on Religious/Social Conservatism. Among students in general, the percentage of high-scorers (16%) is the same as the percentage of low-scorers (16%). And while Roman Catholics include a relatively low percentage of high-scorers (9%), they also include a low percentage of low-scorers (7%). In other words, Catholics are infrequently found at the extremes of Religious/Social Conservatism but are instead bunched up (84%) in the medium level. (A similar tendency to be underrepresented at the extremes of Religious/Social Conservatism is exhibited by students who choose either Eastern Orthodox, Hindu, or United Church of Christ/Congregational as their religious preference.) Catholics show a similar but less pronounced tendency to be underrepresented at the extremes of both Religious Commitment and Religious Engagement.

Most religious groups that are underrepresented at one extreme of religiousness are overrepresented at the other extreme, but Roman Catholics are underrepresented at both extremes. Their being underrepresented at the low end of religiousness may have to do with the fact that in the United States this faith places great emphasis on rituals and practices (attendance at mass and confession, in particular) that are supported by families with strong cultural ties to particular ethnic groups (Irish, Italian, Polish, Mexican, Puerto Rican, and so on). Many such families have historically lived in ethnically homogeneous neighborhoods, where nonparticipation in these rituals and practices is likely to be "noticed." Underrepresentation at the high end of religious-ness may have to do with the relative lack of evangelizing and proselytizing among the Catholic laity. Fewer than half of the Catholic students (42%) say that "being committed to introduc-ing people to my faith" describes them at least "to some extent," compared to large majorities of Baptists (78%), Mormons (76%), and other Christians (63%).

Although the overall decline in frequent church attend-ance during college is 18 percent (from 44% to 25%), there are large discrepancies between denominations. The largest absolute declines are observed among so-called mainline Protestant denominations: Episcopalians (33 percentage points), Methodists (32), Presbyterians (32), and United Church of Christ/ Congregationalists (47). As these same denominations have shown substantial losses in membership over recent decades (see "Trends Among Christians in the U.S.," n.d.), it may well be that these losses are at least partially attributable to the college experi-ence, that is, that the decline in membership in these denomina-tions in the country at large has been fueled in part by the disproportionate drop in attendance at religious services among student members that occurs during the college years.

Since the absolute size of the decline in frequent church attendance is obviously constrained by the 2004 rate—for example, members of a religious group who start college with a frequent attendance rate of 15 percent obviously can't lower their rate by more than 15 percentage points—it may be more informative to assess the decline in attendance in *relative* terms. By this yardstick, Buddhists, Hindus, and Unitarian/Universalists show very large relative declines of 75 percent or more during college, and Baptists, Mormons, Seventh-Day Adventists, and other Christians show relatively small declines of less than 35 percent. In short, it would appear that the conservative, Evangelical faiths show the smallest relative declines in attendance at religious services during college, while the liberal faiths tend to show the largest relative declines.

Roman Catholic students show a moderate absolute decline in frequent attendance at religious services during college, from 55 to 30 percent. In relative terms this represents a 45 percent decline.

Members of only one denomination, Islam, actually show an increase in frequent attendance at religious services (from 26% to 28%) during college. Muslims are also more likely than any other group (39%) to say that "being committed to introducing people to my faith" describes them "to a great extent." In the aftermath of the 9/11 attacks, it is interesting to speculate on the reasons for these unique results. Perhaps Muslim students enrolled in U.S. colleges feel the need to combat negative stereotypes by familiarizing non-Muslims with their faith. Perhaps Muslims who are actively practicing their faith tend to feel uncomfortable in the campus environment and are therefore more likely to associate with fellow practitioners, an inclination that would retard (indeed, reverse) the decline in participation in religious services that we see in other faiths.

ROLE OF COLLEGE TYPE

How do these changes in religious engagement vary by the type of college students attend? As we might suppose, there are substantial differences among different colleges in how religiously engaged their students already are when they first enter college. Not surprisingly, by far the most engaged students are those who enroll in Evangelical colleges, where 90 percent of the entering freshmen have frequently attended religious services in the year prior to enrolling in college (only 1.5% are nonattendees). Next come the students enrolling at other Christian (non-Catholic) colleges (mostly affiliated with mainline Protestant churches), where the precollege rate of frequent attendance at religious services is 61 percent. Frequent attendance among students entering Roman Catholic institutions (49%) is only slightly higher than it is among entering freshmen at private-nonsectarian institutions (44%). Finally, only 39 percent of the entering freshmen at public colleges and universities frequently attend religious services.

The type of college attended also appears to make a difference in how much the student's level of Religious Engagement declines during college. By far the smallest decline is observed at Evangelical colleges, where despite the very high initial level of student engagement—74 percent of the entering freshmen obtain high scores on the Religious Engagement scale and 90 percent attend religious services frequently—there is only a relatively small decline in engagement by the end of the junior year, to 72 percent with high scores and to 76 percent who attend services frequently. Our statistical analyses show that this effect, namely, slowing the overall decline in Religious Engagement that occurs among students in general, can be attributed primarily to one factor: the very high initial level of engagement by the *peer group*, which appears to serve as a brake on the tendency of college students to lower their rate of attendance at religious services after they enter college. So even though a student at an Evangelical college might, like college students elsewhere, be tempted to skip religious services because of other demands associated with being a college student, that student is likely to be deterred by the presence of so many student peers who themselves frequently attend religious services; such peers might well notice the absence of that student at services. Our analyses indicate that once we take into account these peer group effects, the differential effect of Evangelical colleges on Religious Engagement disappears. The capacity of Evangelical colleges to slow the decline in students' level of Religious Engagement that occurs between high school and college thus appears to be entirely attributable to the high level of Religious Engagement that characterizes the student bodies that enroll in these institutions. A similar, but weaker, "braking" effect occurs in Protestant-affiliated institutions.

One other institutional effect bears mentioning here: the tendency for the decline in religious engagement to accelerate among students who attend universities, as opposed to four-year colleges. During the first three years of college the percentage of students with low scores on Religious Engagement increases 6 percent (from 28% to 34%) at universities compared to only 2 percent (from 24% to 26%) at four-year colleges. Our analysis indicates that this difference is at least partly attributable to the fact that university professors, in comparison with the professors teaching in four-year colleges, are much less likely to encourage students to explore religious or spiritual issues. This effect may also be due to the much larger size and impersonality of universities, where there is less personal contact between students and faculty and where any given student's attendance or nonattendance at religious services is less likely to be "noticed."

Summary

Perhaps the best way to understand students' religious development during the college years is to focus on religious engagement and religious/social conservatism. While levels of Religious Commitment show little change after students enter college, we observe sharp declines in Religious/Social Conservatism—especially attitudes toward abortion, casual sex, and atheism—and Religious Engagement, particularly in attendance at religious services. Moreover, the decline in Religious/Social Conservatism is best understood as being attributable to the declines in engagement. Thus, among students who frequently attended religious services in high school, not attending religious services after they enter college can result in a decline in their level of Religious/Social Conservatism.

The decline in levels of Religious Engagement itself can be slowed or even reversed by a number of college activities: joining a campus religious organization, taking a religious studies class, engaging in religious discussions with fellow students or faculty, majoring in education, and having professors who encourage students to explore issues of religion and spirituality. The decline can be accelerated by watching a lot of television, partying and drinking, and majoring in either engineering or social sciences.

These findings on students' religious development during college contrast sharply with the findings on spiritual development. Whereas students' level of Religious Commitment shows little change and their levels of Religious Engagement and Conservatism decline during the college years, four of five indicators of spirituality show positive growth. And while some of the college experiences that strengthen students' religiousness also have positive effects on spirituality, those experiences that have the strongest effects on religiousness show little or no effect on students' spiritual development:

Among the experiences that positively affect both religiousness and spirituality are meditation, self-reflection, donating money to charity, reading sacred texts, reading other spiritual/religious material, engaging in discussions of religion with professors, students, or staff, going on a religious mission trip, and having professors who encourage student discussions of religious/spiritual matters.

Experiences that have the strongest positive effects on religiousness but less effect (or no effect) on spirituality include praying, attending religious services, religious singing/chanting, and participating in a campus religious organization. Also, drinking and partying are negatively associated with growth in religiousness but unrelated to spiritual growth.

Finally, we have identified several other experiences that positively affect spiritual development but have little or no effect on religiousness: study abroad, leadership training, interracial interaction, taking interdisciplinary courses, taking service learning courses, talking with faculty outside of class, and having professors who encourage students to explore questions of meaning and purpose.

CHAPTER SEVEN

RELIGIOUS STRUGGLE
AND SKEPTICISM

We turn now to consider two qualities that play an important role in many students' religious development: Religious Struggle and Religious Skepticism. In this chapter we shall see how each of these qualities changes during the college years, and examine various aspects of the undergraduate experience that help to shape them.

RELIGIOUS STRUGGLE

For many students the college years are a time for reflection about one's faith: What do I really believe? What is the meaning of life? Why is there suffering, evil, and death in the world? A number of studies have documented the extent to which such religious struggles are paramount in students' minds and how such questions and struggles affect their well-being (Johnson and Hayes, 2003; Pargament et al., 2005).

In focus group sessions and individual interviews that we conducted with undergraduates, we found that many students do indeed struggle over reconciling the teachings of their faith traditions with their experience and with their evolving beliefs. Exposure to college appears to challenge their beliefs as they encounter other faiths and beliefs. College is also a time of dealing with major life events and decisions, such as choosing one's life work and deciding about plans after college: What kind of career path should I follow? Should I go to work right after college or should I pursue graduate or professional school? How one's faith and prayers may or may not inform such decisions can be a source of struggle. In many of our interviews we found that students question whether prayer can help them with major life decisions or whether God could play a role or affect the course of their lives. Many students find themselves troubled by questions such as how to reconcile a loving God with the death of friends or close family members, or with major disasters and wars. As one student told us, "When I see people hurt, I think that's when I question God."

Students' struggles also center on their relationship to God: "How do I love God?" "How do I know exactly what's good? Is it because my parents told me I should do this and not that?" "What does it actually mean to be pure?" "How can mine be the only true faith when there are so many other students who believe differently?"

While there can be negative consequences of religious struggle, there is also evidence that such struggles can have positive effects on overall growth, and that a crisis in faith can be both necessary and instrumental in promoting personal growth and maturation (Hill and Pargament, 2003; Pargament et al., 2005).

Evolution of Religious Struggle During College

Recall from Chapter Two that Religious Struggle is a composite measure of responses to seven individual items in the survey questionnaire:

Feeling unsettled about spiritual and religious matters
Feeling disillusioned with [my] religious upbringing
Struggled to understand evil, suffering, and death
Questioned [my] religious/spiritual beliefs
Felt angry with God
Felt distant from God
Disagreed with [my] family about religious matters

Students' overall level of Religious Struggle increased between 2004 and 2007, with the number of high-scorers rising from 9 to 13 percent. Five of the seven items in this scale show increased endorsement over the three years: "struggled to understand evil, suffering, and death" (agreement increased from 64% to 70%); "questioned [my] religious/spiritual beliefs" (from 56% to 61%); "feeling disillusioned with my religious upbringing" (from 7% to 10%); "feeling unsettled about spiritual and religious matters" (from 14% to 17%); and "felt distant from God" (from 64% to 66%). That students become more likely to question their religious and spiritual beliefs and to report that they struggle to understand evil in the world is perhaps to be expected, given that being in college exposes them to new ideas, new faith traditions, a new and often more culturally diverse peer group, and more opportunities to reflect and question aspects of their own faith and belief systems. As one of the students we interviewed said, "That's probably my big issue; how do all those old beliefs fit into my new ones, and how can I shape them to make them fit with who I am now?"

The final two items in the Religious Struggle scale show small declines in the number of high-scorers: "felt angry with God" (from 45% to 43%) and "disagreed with my family about religious matters" (from 50% to 47%). Changes in this last item could well be attributable to the reduced contact with family that most students experience when they attend college. The slight decline in feeling angry with God is somewhat more puzzling in light of the students' greater sense of "distance" from God and their increasing struggle with issues of evil, suffering, and death. One possible explanation is that feeling less angry reflects growing maturity on the part of students, as well as their greater sense of equanimity (see Chapter Four).

Comparing changes in levels of Religious Struggle between the freshman and junior years by the types of colleges students are enrolled in, we see rising levels of struggle across all institutional types, with the greatest increase occurring among students attending Evangelical colleges: from 7 percent reporting high levels as freshmen to 17 percent reporting high levels as juniors. Given that more than seven in ten students who attend Evangelical colleges identify themselves as Evangelical Christians, it may well be that many of these students have had a relatively sheltered religious upbringing, where friends and family alike embrace a common belief system and where there are sanctions against questioning one's beliefs (this conclusion is consistent with the finding that Evangelical college students, compared to students enrolling in other types of colleges, show the lowest level of Religious Struggle, 7%, when they *start* college). For many Evangelical college students, being in college may thus represent their first sustained experience in critical thinking, where ideas, regardless of their source, are subjected to investigation, discussion, argument, and debate. Assuming that theological propositions also come up for critical examination in such an environment, the experience could well be unsettling and possibly even disorienting for some of these students, leading them in turn to begin questioning their belief systems and their faith in general. As one student at an Evangelical institution told us: "One [thing] I've been thinking again about lately is, just what exactly is the nature of faith? Is it simply something that you have when you don't understand something? Is it something that you have when you fully understand something? And how do we define faith as it relates to our understanding of God, or our beliefs?"

Students who attend Evangelical institutions also show unique patterns of change in certain scale items. For example, whereas 2 percent fewer students overall report "feeling angry with God" after three years of college, students at Evangelical colleges show a 12 percent increase during the same period. Likewise, while fewer juniors in the total sample, compared to when they were freshmen, tell us that they "disagree with family members about religious matters," students at Evangelical colleges show the opposite trend: more report religious disagreements with family as juniors than as freshmen. Indeed, among students attending Evangelical colleges, every item in the scale changes in the direction of greater struggle, again indicating that the college experience may create more religious struggle for students attending Evangelical colleges, most of whom self-identify as Evangelical Christians. This finding further reinforces our interest in exploring what it is about the overall college experience that might be exacerbating students' religious struggles.

The religious groups that evidence the highest levels of Religious Struggle as college juniors include Quakers and Seventh-Day Adventists, with 24 and 22 percent, respectively, reporting high levels of struggle. Even though many Seventh-Day Adventists are strongly committed to their faith (see Chapter Six), the fact that they also evidence a relatively high level of Religious Struggle may have to do with church doctrine, which speaks of "Adventist values of freedom of worship and belief" and states that "What we choose to believe and how we choose to worship should be according to the dictates of our conscience" ("Seventh Day Adventist Church," n.d.). In a similar fashion, many Quakers view "true religion as a personal encounter with God, rather than ritual and ceremony" and "do not regard the Bible as the only source of belief and conduct. They rely upon their Inner Light to resolve what they perceive as the Bible's many contradictions. They also feel free to take advantage of scientific and philosophical findings from other sources" ("Religious Society of Friends," n.d.). In short, such reliance on personal judgment and critical thinking in matters of faith could well increase the chances that Quakers and Seventh-Day Adventists might experience religious struggle.

By contrast, students who adhere to an Eastern Orthodox faith, Jewish students, Mormons, and Lutherans report the lowest levels of Religious Struggle (only 7% or fewer obtain high scores). What these diverse faiths have in common that might minimize the amount of religious struggle that they experience is not clear.

ROLE OF COLLEGE EXPERIENCE

What accounts for student changes with respect to their level of Religious Struggle? Can specific experiences with peers, faculty, curricula, and cocurricula result in students having more struggles with faith?

Our study findings reveal that the student's peer group can affect the individual student's degree of Religious Struggle in two ways. First, religious struggle appears to be contagious in the sense that we observe relatively large increases in Religious Struggle on campuses where a high proportion of the student's peers are experiencing religious struggle when they start college (the Evangelical colleges being a notable exception). Second, on campuses where peers are heavily engaged in religious practices— attending religious service, praying, reading sacred texts—there also tends to be relatively large increases in Religious Struggle during college. These findings are consistent with a large body of earlier research showing that peer culture can have a strong effect on students' beliefs and behaviors (Astin, 1993; Pascarella and Terenzini, 2005). Students who struggle and who share these struggles with friends and classmates may well experience disequilibrium in their faith and begin to question aspects of their faith. One would also expect that a student's religious struggle would more likely intensify if he finds himself in the presence of a highly religiously engaged peer group. That is, seeing most of one's peers attending church regularly and praying frequently may well upset a student who is beginning to question her relationship to her faith. (The fact that Evangelical college students, compared to students entering other types of colleges, display by far the highest level of Religious Engagement when they begin college helps to explain why they show such a large increase in religious struggle, despite their initially low level of struggle.)

A major field can also affect students' religious struggles. For example, religious struggles appear to be heightened when students major in English, other humanities fields, the fine arts, or social sciences; majoring in one of these fields increases the likelihood that students will question their religious and spiritual beliefs, feel unsettled about spiritual and religious matters, or feel disillusioned with their religious upbringing. By contrast, students' religious struggles are relatively unlikely to intensify when they major in business.

In the humanities and social sciences fields, students are likely to be exposed to ideas and values that differ from those they held prior to coming to college. Such fields may encourage students to think critically, to question received wisdom, and to consider diverse points of view with respect to historical, social, or philosophical perspectives. Such experiences may in turn cause students to raise questions about the validity of their own faith and belief systems.

A number of other college experiences appear to increase students' level of Religious Struggle. Students are more likely to report more religious struggle as juniors than they did as freshmen if they frequently discuss religion with faculty, staff, or peers, and especially if their professors encourage them to explore spiritual issues. This latter variable is a composite measure made up of three individual items: professors encouraged discussions of religious/spiritual matters; encouraged personal expressions of spirituality; and acted as spiritual models. Apparently, uncertainties about one's faith tend to increase when a student's professors actively encourage exploration of matters of faith and spirituality. Two other academic experiences also appear to exacerbate students' religious struggles: study abroad, and taking interdisciplinary courses. Students who participate in a study abroad program show a 6 percent increase in high-scorers on Religious Struggle during college, compared to only a 2 percent increase among those who do not participate. A similar difference is found between students who do and do not take interdisciplinary courses. Finally, we note that increases in Religious Struggle also tend to be larger than average among students who are highly engaged in their academic work (as reflected in the amount of studying and homework they do).

In short, it appears that religious struggle tends to be greater if students are academically engaged or if they find themselves encountering cultural diversity (study abroad) or disciplinary diversity (interdisciplinary courses). Such experiences may not only raise students' consciousness about differences and inequities but also encourage them to think globally and to appreciate how interconnected we all are. Under such conditions, it is perhaps to be expected that some students will begin to question traditional beliefs: How can there be only one true faith or church? Does God favor only one faith to the exclusion of all others? Such questioning could in turn lead some students to begin feeling unsettled in their beliefs, or disillusioned with their religious upbringing.

While questioning one's longstanding beliefs can be unsettling or even precipitate a spiritual crisis, such questioning may also have positive effects in that students may embark on a period of deeper self-exploration and, at the same time, become more aware, and more accepting, of the diversity of religious traditions. Such an interpretation is consistent with the strong positive association between Religious Struggle and Charitable Involvement (helping friends with personal problems, and giving money to charity). Our data suggest that this relationship may operate in both directions: experiencing religious struggle seems to increase the odds that students will exhibit caring behaviors, such as helping friends with problems and giving money to charity; and engaging in such charitable activities tends to heighten students' religious struggles. Here it should be noted that simply becoming more aware of the suffering of others can lead students to experience a disconnect between the idea of a loving and protective God, on the one hand, and the pain and suffering in the world, on the other.

Greater levels of Religious Struggle are also associated with watching a lot of television and a frequent consumption of alcohol. Again, the cause is unclear, although we must consider the possibility that television viewing and drinking are mechanisms that students may use to avoid the discomfort they feel as a result of their religious struggles.

Such an interpretation is consistent with two other findings: that students' religious struggles can be intensified if they experience either a serious personal injury or illness, or if they experience the death of a close friend or family member while they are enrolled in college. It is not surprising that such feelings of doubt and struggle would occur when as a result of their experiences of loss and pain students perceive God as a punisher and not as a protector or a loving and caring God. As one student said, poignantly: "When my mom was getting sick I started questioning, 'Why is this happening to my mom? Why is she going through that when she's been good throughout her life, and there are people who are stealing and killing, and they are fine?'" Or as another student told us: "My dad passed away [recently], and it really affected me to the point where I wasn't sure what I believed. I really wasn't sure how I wanted to live my life, or what I wanted to do."

Such struggles can sometimes prove to be almost overwhelming, as suggested by this student interviewee: "I feel like sometimes my struggles are just too powerful. I can't get over them; I just feel so defeated. I've felt so lost. I've felt like I have nowhere to go."

Our data suggest that such self-reflection as well as meditation can exacerbate a student's religious struggles. Undergraduates who engage in self-reflection on a daily basis show a 6 percent increase in high-scorers on Religious Struggle, as compared to only a 2–3 percent increase among those who reflect less frequently. Again, we cannot be sure about the direction of this relationship: the fact that a student is engaged in a religious struggle could lead that student to engage in self-reflection, yet self-reflection may also lead some students to begin questioning their religious faith. The latter interpretation is consistent with the finding that 35 percent of students endorsed the statement, "It is difficult to reconcile the existence of a loving God with all the pain and suffering in the world."

To summarize, the pattern of college experiences that appear to promote religious struggle is somewhat different from the patterns we have observed with other religious and spiritual qualities. While alcohol consumption and frequent television viewing are negatively associated with several other religious and spiritual measures, they are associated with higher levels of Religious Struggle. And while increases in Religious Struggle are associated with having a serious illness or injury, or experiencing the death of a close friend or family member, these experiences are generally not associated with changes in other religious or spiritual qualities. At the same time, we find that engaging in frequent self-reflection is positively associated both with increases in Religious Struggle and with growth in spiritual qualities.

RELIGIOUS SKEPTICISM

Religious Skepticism is in many respects the polar opposite of Religious Commitment and Religious Engagement as described in the previous chapter. Religious commitment and engagement are typically based on a belief in the truth of particular theological propositions; religious skepticism, on the belief that these same propositions are in error. It comes as little surprise then that our measure of Religious Skepticism is negatively correlated with our measures of Religious Commitment and Religious Engagement.[1]

During the college years, Religious Skepticism shows very little overall change, with the number of high-scorers increasing slightly from 19 to 20 percent. However, this apparent lack of change masks substantial changes in some of the individual items making up this scale. Two items in particular show relatively large changes in the direction of greater skepticism: "It doesn't matter what I believe as long as I lead a moral life" (agreement grows from 51%

to 58%); and "While science can provide important information about the physical world, only religion can truly explain existence" (*dis*agreement increases from 46% to 52%). These two items alone account for the slight net increase in overall Religious Skepticism. In fact, changes in six of the other seven items in this scale actually suggest decreased skepticism. The largest declines are associated with three items: "I have never felt a sense of sacredness" (agreement declines from 30% to 27%); "In the future, science will be able to explain everything" (agreement declines from 30% to 27%); and increased "belief in life after death" (50% to 52%). The remaining four items in the Religious Skepticism scale show changes of less than 1 percent. Several of the larger changes—that leading a moral life doesn't necessarily depend on having particular religious beliefs, and the rejection of the idea that either science or religion alone can explain everything—suggest the development of a more ecumenical worldview, changes that may result from being exposed to more diverse points of view and faith traditions during the college years.

As one of our student interviewees put it: "Science basically throws up its hands when a discussion is raised about the origins of the universe. There is something that exists on a higher level; there may be some sort of physical reason why the universe exists, but also a spiritual reason for that physical condition."

There are wide differences in the degree of religious skepticism expressed by students depending on their religious preference. By far the most skeptical college juniors are those with no religious preference (68% obtain high scores on this scale), followed by Unitarian/Universalists (53%), Jews (41%), and Buddhists (34%). The least skeptical students—all with fewer than 6 percent high-scorers—are Hindus, Muslims, Baptists, other (predominantly nondenominational) Christians, and members of the Church of Christ. (The latter three groups include large numbers of Evangelical Christians.) During college, Baptists show significant declines in skepticism, while Jews show significant increases.

Students with no religious affiliation often express their skepticism in the form of indifference. As one of our student interviewees put it: "I've never really tried to grapple with, Is there a God, or not? Is there a higher being? I think it's just there, and I don't really pay any attention to it, because I do not feel like it's relevant to me."

Sometimes skepticism is fostered by personal experiences within particular faith traditions: "Junior year in high school through sophomore year in college was not necessarily doubt—'I don't believe in God'—but it was more kind of, 'I'm frustrated with what people were preaching and how they were living their life. And so it was really easy for me to disconnect. When I saw these inconsistencies, it was easy for me to just kind of separate myself."

When we compare different types of colleges, once again the Evangelical colleges show a unique pattern. Not only do these colleges enroll the least skeptical students of all college types (only 2% of their freshmen score high on Religious Skepticism), but their students are also the only ones who show a net decline in skepticism (to 1% high-scorers) during the college years. Apparently, the large increase in religious struggle evidenced by Evangelical college students (see earlier) does not seem to have contributed to greater religious skepticism.

College Experiences That Affect Skepticism

By far the most powerful influence on religious skepticism during the college years is religious engagement. This effect is of course a negative one, the highest levels of skepticism being associated with the lowest levels of engagement. Students who never pray, for example, show a 13 percent increase in high-scorers on Religious Skepticism between the time they enter college as freshmen and the end of their junior year, compared to a 2 percent decline among those who pray at least several times a week. Similarly, students who never attend religious services show a 6 percent increase in high-scorers on Religious Skepticism during college, compared to a 3 percent decrease among those who attend frequently. Finally, participating in a campus religious organization is also associated with reduced Religious Skepticism: participants show a 3 percent decline in high-scorers on Religious Skepticism, compared to a 3 percent increase among students who do not participate in such organizations. Clearly, these three forms of religious engagement all help to minimize religious skepticism by reinforcing the student's religious beliefs.

One other experience turns out to dampen levels of Religious Skepticism: participation in intercollegiate football or basketball (the so-called revenue sports). This is consistent with what we reported in the previous chapter, namely, that participation in these sports tends to have a positive effect on religious/social conservatism. Again, given the frequent participation of such teams in religious or quasi-religious activities such as group prayer, one would expect there to be sanctions against expressions of religious skepticism by individual team members.

A diverse set of activities and experiences turns out to be associated with increased levels of Religious Skepticism: partying, alcohol consumption, watching television, study abroad, participation in ROTC, and having parents go through a separation or divorce. Partying and drinking, of course, are negatively related to growth in religiousness (Chapter Six), and watching television is negatively related to growth in spirituality (Chapter Five), but study abroad is positively related to growth in two spiritual measures, Ethic of Caring and Ecumenical Worldview. Study abroad may well contribute to religious skepticism by exposing students to a wide range of religious believers and nonbelievers in other countries. The fact that parents are becoming separated or divorced may contribute to some students' sense of cynicism about their religious faith. Finally, the positive effect of participation in ROTC on Religious Skepticism presents something of an interpretive challenge. Although only about 1 percent of our students are ROTC participants, the difference in growth in skepticism is substantial: during college, ROTC participants show a 14 percent increase in highly skeptical students, compared to only a 1 percent increase among nonparticipants. What it is about the ROTC experience that might account for this difference remains unclear.

There is one characteristic of the peer environment that turns out to influence the level of Religious Skepticism: the political orientation of the student body. Specifically, students tend to become more skeptical if they attend a college where their peers are politically liberal, and less skeptical if they enroll in a college with a politically conservative student body. This pattern is consistent with what we know about the relationship between religion and politics, that is, that politically conservative students tend to be much more religious than are politically liberal students. So, attending a college where peers are politically conservative would tend to discourage the development of religious skepticism, whereas attending a college where the students are politically liberal would be more likely to encourage religious skepticism.

Note that several of the same experiences that proved to have an effect on the development of Religious Skepticism (prayer, partying, drinking, joining a campus religious organization, being a member of a revenue-sports team) were shown earlier (Chapter Six) to have the opposite effect on Religious Commitment and/or Religious/Social Conservatism. Given the strong negative correlations between skepticism and these other two measures—highly skeptical students tend to score low on Religious Commitment and Religious/Social Conservatism—such a result is to be expected. Therefore, college experiences that foster religious skepticism tend to have negative effects on religious commitment and religious/social conservatism, while experiences that enhance the latter two qualities tend to diminish the development of religious skepticism.

SUMMARY

Although religious struggle and religious skepticism seem to have a good deal in common, our data suggest that they are quite distinctive phenomena. Thus, while highly skeptical students tend to be nonreligious, students who are heavily engaged in a religious struggle are often highly religious. This distinction is well illustrated in the case of the Evangelical colleges. When they first enroll at such colleges, Evangelical students display lower scores on both Skepticism and Struggle than do students at any other type of institution. However, during college, the two measures diverge: Evangelical college students show larger increases in Religious Struggle than do students at any other type of institution, while simultaneously showing declines in Skepticism. By contrast, students at all other types of college show increases in their levels of Skepticism during their college years.

While a few college experiences affect religious struggle and religious skepticism similarly—increased struggle and skepticism are both associated with watching television, drinking, and study abroad—most of the key experiences affect one quality differently from the other. Meditation and self-reflection, for example, both promote struggle but not skepticism, while religious engagement (especially prayer) diminishes skepticism markedly, but struggle only marginally. Experiencing the death of a close friend or family member contributes to the students' religious struggles but not to their religious skepticism, while a divorce or separation of the students' parents promotes religious skepticism but not religious struggle.

CHAPTER EIGHT

HOW SPIRITUAL GROWTH AFFECTS EDUCATIONAL AND PERSONAL DEVELOPMENT

Our focus up to this point has been on the growth of spirituality and religiousness during the college years and on how that growth is affected by different types of college experiences. This approach, in effect, treats spirituality and religiousness as college *outcomes*. However, a skeptic might look over these findings and comment: "It's all well and good to know how students' spiritual and religious attributes change during college and how different college experiences promote or inhibit these changes, but what about the other outcomes of college? What about the student's academic performance, leadership skills, psychological well-being, and satisfaction with college? Does the student's religious or spiritual development have any impact on these more "traditional" outcomes of college? And if we were to implement some of the educational practices and programs that were found to foster spiritual growth, what would be the consequences for these same traditional outcomes?"

Our data suggest that spiritual growth does indeed enhance many of these other college outcomes. In this chapter we explore some of these positive effects of spiritual development in detail. We pose two basic questions: First, if students manage to achieve significant growth during college in spiritual qualities such as equanimity, does this improve their academic performance in college, raise their educational aspirations, strengthen their leadership skills, or enhance their satisfaction with the college experience? Second, if colleges and universities decide to put greater emphasis on self-reflection, interdisciplinary studies, and other practices that promote spiritual development, how would these same traditional outcomes be affected?

To explore such questions, we obviously need to devise measures of the more traditional college outcomes. For simplicity we have organized these outcomes into three groups: *intellectual/academic, personal/emotional,* and *attitudinal.* We employ a total of eight such traditional outcomes, including:

intellectual/academic outcomes
- grades in college
- educational aspirations
- intellectual self-esteem

personal/emotional outcomes
- psychological well-being
- leadership abilities and skills
- satisfaction with college

attitudinal outcomes
- growth in the ability to get along with people of different races and cultures
- growth in the importance placed on promoting racial understanding

We selected the last two outcomes in recognition of a rapidly changing global, multicultural society and of the importance that many colleges assign to developing students' awareness and understanding of cultural differences.

IMPACT OF SPIRITUAL AND RELIGIOUS GROWTH ON COLLEGE OUTCOMES

To simplify the task of assessing how spiritual growth affects these more traditional college outcomes, we selected a representative subgroup of three spiritual measures: Spiritual Quest, Equanimity, and Global Citizenship (the last combining Ethic of

Caring and Ecumenical Worldview); and two religious measures: Religious Struggle and Religious Engagement (the latter being strongly associated with Religious Commitment, Religious/Social Conservatism, and Religious Skepticism). The basic goal of these analyses was to determine whether changes in these five spiritual/religious measures during the college years are associated with any of the eight more traditional outcomes. These analyses were designed to test the effects of changes in these spiritual/religious measures only after all other variables—entering-freshman characteristics, college experiences, and so on—had been controlled. For details see the Appendix.

INTELLECTUAL/ACADEMIC OUTCOMES

Academic development is surely among the most fundamental and essential goals of undergraduate education. For this particular study our interest is in how students perform in their courses, as reflected in their overall grade point average (GPA) at the end of their junior year. We looked to see if they performed better or worse academically during the first three years in college compared to how they performed in high school. A second intellectual/academic outcome consisted of students' motivation for further education, as reflected in their intent to pursue an advanced degree. The final index of intellectual/academic growth consisted of a scale we created to assess students' intellectual self-esteem. (To create this latter measure, we combined the responses to five items in the questionnaire that addressed their sense of self relative to persons their own age. These items included their sense of academic ability; writing and mathematical abilities; intellectual self-confidence; and their drive to achieve.) Since all three of these measures of students' intellectual/academic development were assessed at the time of college entry in Fall 2004 and again in Spring 2007 at the end of their junior year, we were able to measure change during the college years.

As far as academic performance is concerned, there is a substantial drop in students' GPAs from high school to after three years of college. Grade averages of "A" decline by half—from 30 to 15 percent—and grade averages of "B" or lower nearly double—from 25 to 48 percent. This decline in GPA is not all that surprising, as high school work is generally less demanding intellectually in comparison to college. High school students who go on to college are a select group academically, and when they get to college they have to compete with others of similarly high ability and motivation.

When it comes to students' degree aspirations, there are net declines over three years in college in the number of students who plan to obtain Ph.D.s (−3%) or medical degrees (−3%), and corresponding increases in the numbers who are seeking law degrees (+1%), master's degrees (+3%), or bachelor's degrees (+1%). Overall, it appears that after three years in college, students' aspirations for higher degrees become more realistic, perhaps because they may begin to appreciate the high intellectual demands and performance expectations of advanced graduate study and medical school.

Finally, although overall scores on intellectual self-esteem increase only slightly between the freshman and junior years, the individual self-rating items that constitute the intellectual self-esteem measure show opposing trends: after three years of college, students rate themselves higher in academic ability, writing ability, and intellectual self-esteem, but lower in mathematical ability and drive to achieve. The decline in math self-confidence is consistent with other evidence suggesting a net decline in math competence during the college years (Astin, 1993). The decline in drive to achieve, as well as in aspirations for medical and doctorate degrees, may reflect a "cooling out" of the optimistic expectations that typify many new college freshmen.

We turn now to consider how our three outcomes are affected by spiritual and religious growth during the first three years of college. Because one of the key questions of this study was to ask how spirituality or religiousness might affect academic and intellectual growth, our analyses examined whether changes in religiousness and spirituality over the first three years in college play a role in students' academic performance, their feelings about the importance of pursuing further education, and their assessment of their intellectual abilities. Specifically, we examined the effects of five of the measures of students' religiousness and spirituality, as described above: Equanimity, Religious Engagement, Religious Struggle, Spiritual Quest (four of these measures are described in more detail in Chapter Two), and a new measure that we call "Global Citizenship," which combines elements of two closely related measures, Ethic of Caring and Ecumenical Worldview. (We created the Global Citizenship measure to simplify the presentation of findings, as preliminary analyses indicated that results from separate analyses of Ethic of Caring and Ecumenical Worldview would be very similar. Global Citizenship, which has an Alpha reliability of .80, is based on six items: "Trying to change things that are unfair in the world"; "Reducing pain and suffering in the world"; "Feeling a strong connection to all of humanity"; "Improving my understanding of other countries and cultures"; "Improving the human condition"; and "Helping others who are in difficulty.")

When it comes to the college GPA, the most striking finding concerns the spiritual quality of equanimity: *when college students show significant growth in equanimity, their GPAs tend to improve.* For example, if we look only at the 3,578 students who started college with a medium level of Equanimity and an average high school grade of either B+ or A–, 63 percent of those who increased their Equanimity level after entering college were able to maintain at least a B+ average in college, compared to only 42 percent of those whose Equanimity declined. (Among those who maintained their medium Equanimity level during college, 55% earned at least a B+ average in college.) As it turns out, this is the only spiritual/religious quality that has an effect on college GPA. Growth in equanimity also has a positive effect on the student's intellectual self-esteem (see below), which raises an interesting question: does equanimity enhance intellectual self-esteem by improving the student's GPA, or does it improve GPA by enhancing self-esteem? Although we cannot answer this question for certain, it would be an interesting issue for future research.

Equanimity, it will be recalled, reflects the extent to which the student feels at peace and centered, is able to find meaning in times of hardship, and feels good about the direction of her life. It is thus not surprising that an increase in the student's level of Equanimity during the college years would have positive effects on his self-confidence and academic performance. Students who lack equanimity would be more likely to expend psychic energy in futile ways and to feel anxious about or overwhelmed by their academic work. Growth in equanimity during the college years shows a positive effect on the student's intellectual self-esteem. For example, if we look only at students who started college with medium scores on both Equanimity and intellectual self-esteem, those whose level of Equanimity increased during college, compared to those whose Equanimity scores declined, were three times more likely (27% vs. 9%) to score high on intellectual self-esteem by the end of their junior year.

Intellectual self-esteem scores are also positively affected by growth in another spiritual measure, Spiritual Quest, although the effect is not as strong as in the case with Equanimity. Spiritual Quest is a measure that assesses students' interest in searching for meaning and purpose in life, and finding answers to life's great mysteries. We can only speculate on the meaning of this result, but such spiritual searching would seem to go hand in hand with academic engagement more generally, since it implies an active mind that searches for truth and understanding.

Somewhat surprisingly, students' aspirations for graduate study turn out to be negatively affected by growth in levels of Religious Engagement. As described in Chapter Six, Religious Engagement comprises behaviors such as attending religious services, praying, and reading sacred texts. It's not clear why becoming more religiously engaged during college should weaken students' motivation to pursue further education. One possibility is that being highly engaged religiously and accepting unquestioningly the dogmas of one's faith tradition convinces some students that there is no need to pursue further education. At the same time, the positivistic mind-set that often characterizes the intellectual approach of many college and university faculty may serve to alienate some highly religious students and cause them to forgo graduate study, which ordinarily involves much more intense and prolonged contact with faculty members than does undergraduate education.

Growth in levels of Global Citizenship, in contrast, tends to increase the likelihood that the student will aspire to education beyond the baccalaureate degree. Global Citizenship, a measure that combines items from our Ethic of Caring and Ecumenical Worldview scales, reflects the student's concern about helping others and one's identification with the global community. It includes items such as trying to change things that are unfair in the world, reducing pain and suffering in the world, and feeling a strong connection to all humanity. The fact that growth in this quality tends to raise students' educational aspirations suggests that expanding one's understanding of and commitment to global issues and strengthening one's sense of caring for others may spur an interest in pursuing further education as a means of positioning oneself to make a difference in the world.

In sum, these findings, which show the positive role that spirituality can play in academic development, underscore the importance of assisting students to grow and develop in all of the important dimensions of self, not just academically but also spiritually.

PERSONAL/EMOTIONAL OUTCOMES

To examine how spiritual development interfaces with students' personal and emotional development, we examined three outcomes: psychological well-being, self-rated leadership skills and abilities, and satisfaction with college. "Psychological well-being" includes the following items: *not* feeling "depressed," *not* feeling "overwhelmed by everything I have to do," and *not* feeling that "my life is filled with stress and anxiety,"[1] as well as the student's self-assessment of his or her "emotional health." Combining these items into one measure, we find that as freshmen, 33 percent of students receive high scores on psychological well-being and only 7 percent score low (see Chapter Two and the Appendix for more on how we determined high and low scores). The follow-up survey we conducted at the end of their junior year indicates that *students' level of psychological well-being declines during the college years,* with the number of high-scorers falling from 33 to 21 percent and the number of low-scorers rising from 7 to 12 percent. Between their freshman and junior years the number frequently feeling that "my life is filled with stress and anxiety" increases from 26 to 42 percent; frequently feeling "overwhelmed by all I have to do" increases from 32 to 46 percent; and frequently feeling "depressed" increases from 9 to 12 percent, while the number rating themselves "below average" on "emotional health" increases from 10 to 14 percent. Clearly, the greater academic demands of college, coupled with the pressures of trying to balance school, a job, and a personal life, take a toll on students' sense of psychological well-being.

"Leadership" is a self-concept measure comprising the student's self-rating on six traits that are often exhibited by persons in leadership roles: social self-confidence, understanding of others, self-understanding, cooperativeness, leadership ability, and public speaking ability (Higher Education Research Institute, 1996; Komives, Lucas, and McMahon, 2006; Kouzes and Posner, 1993). Students in general tend to rate themselves high on all these traits, both as freshmen and as juniors, with the number rating themselves "above average" ranging from 35 to 69 percent, depending on the trait. With the exception of cooperativeness, the percentages of above-average self-ratings on these traits grow by an average of about 3 points between the freshman and junior years. Cooperativeness drops by 2 percentage points. Such changes indicate that many students feel that their leadership qualities have grown during college, a trend that could be attributed to the many extracurricular opportunities that college offers students to develop leadership skills and behaviors.

"Satisfaction" is a single item asking students how satisfied they are with their college experience. About half the students (48%) report being "very" satisfied with college, with another 43 percent saying that they are "somewhat" satisfied. Of course, this high rate of satisfaction comes from students who did not drop out of college and who managed to progress successfully from freshman to junior years in three years. If we were to include dropouts and students who leave college temporarily in our sample, the overall satisfaction level would no doubt be lower.

Significant effects on these three personal/emotional outcomes were associated with growth on all of the spiritual and religious measures except Global Citizenship. Once again, Equanimity proves to have positive effects, in this case on all three measures of students' personal/emotional development: psychological well-being, leadership, and satisfaction with college. In other words, those students who show substantial growth in equanimity during the undergraduate years also benefit in terms of a greater sense of psychological well-being, greater-than-average development of leadership skills, and higher levels of satisfaction

FIGURE 8.1.   EFFECT OF CHANGES IN EQUANIMITY ON SATISFACTION WITH COLLEGE

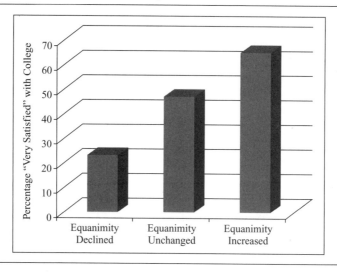

Note: Based on 7,800 undergraduates with "medium" scores on Equanimity as freshmen.

with their college experience. The size of the effects on psychological well-being and satisfaction are especially striking: among students who started college with medium scores on both Equanimity and psychological well-being, those whose Equanimity scores increased during college were much more likely to report high levels of psychological well-being at the end of their junior year (24%) than were those whose Equanimity scores declined (6%). Similarly, students whose Equanimity scores increased after they entered college, compared with those whose scores declined, expressed a much higher level of being "very satisfied" with their college experience: 65 versus 23 percent (see Figure 8.1). Since the quality of equanimity reflects the ability of students to find meaning in times of hardship, feel at peace and centered, and feel good about the direction in which their lives are headed, it is no surprise that this spiritual quality can play a positive role in the development of students' sense of psychological well-being and satisfaction with college.

While growth in levels of Spiritual Quest also had a weak positive effect on the development of leadership abilities, it shows negative effects on the other two personal/emotional measures, psychological well-being and satisfaction with college. Keeping in mind that Spiritual Quest reflects students' strivings to attain inner harmony, become a more loving person, find meaning and purpose in life, and find answers to the mysteries of life, it may well be that engaging in such a search can at times prove to be frustrating and emotionally unsettling to a point where psychological well-being and satisfaction are negatively affected.

Religious Struggle proves to have negative effects on all three personal/emotional measures. That is, students whose religious struggles intensify during the college years also tend to show less satisfaction with college, below-average growth in leadership skills, and diminished psychological well-being. These effects are perhaps to be expected in light of the fact that Religious Struggle is defined by items such as feeling unsettled about religious and spiritual matters, questioning one's religious beliefs, and struggling to understand evil, suffering, and death.

One final finding has to do with Religious Engagement, which turned out to have a weak negative effect on satisfaction with college. One can only speculate on the meaning of this result. Given that students in general tend to become less religiously engaged after entering college (see Chapter Six), it could be the case that those students who "buck the trend" by maintaining a high level of engagement after enrolling in college find themselves increasingly alienated because most of their classmates are no longer as religiously engaged as they are. This is another finding that bears further investigation.

ATTITUDINAL OUTCOMES

We employed two attitudinal measures in the 2007 follow-up survey, which were designed to reflect growth in students' awareness and understanding of cultural differences and of the emerging global society: students' self-assessed growth since entering college in the "ability to get along with people of different races and cultures"; and the importance that students assign to "helping to promote racial understanding." The second item was also pretested in the 2004 freshman survey.

By far the strongest effects of any of the spiritual/religious measures on these attitudinal outcomes are associated with growth in levels of Global Citizenship. The greater the growth in Global Citizenship, the more likely the student is to endorse the promotion of racial understanding, and to report significant growth in his or her ability to get along with different races and cultures. To get an idea of the strength of these effects, look at Figure 8.2, which shows only those students who started college with a medium level of Global Citizenship and a marginal commitment—reflected in their response of "somewhat important"—to a personal goal of promoting racial understanding. Among those whose level of Global Citizenship increases (from medium to high) after entering college, more than two-thirds (71%) also increase their level of commitment to the goal of promoting racial understanding (to "very important" or "essential"). By contrast, fewer than one in seven (13%) of those

FIGURE 8.2. EFFECT OF CHANGES IN GLOBAL CITIZENSHIP ON COMMITMENT
TO THE GOAL OF RACIAL UNDERSTANDING

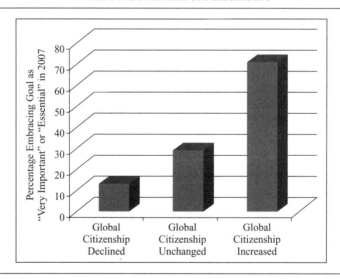

Note: Based on 3,466 undergraduates with "medium" 2004 scores on Global Citizenship who indicated in 2004 that promoting racial understanding was a "somewhat important" goal.

whose level of Global Citizenship declines during college (from medium to low) raise their level of commitment to promoting racial understanding.

The reasons for these effects become clear when we review the content of our Global Citizenship measure. As mentioned earlier, Global Citizenship combines elements of two other spiritual measures, Ethic of Caring and Ecumenical Worldview, by incorporating personal goals such as "trying to change things that are unfair in the world," "improving the human condition," "improving my understanding of other countries and cultures," and "feeling a strong connection to all humanity."

Students whose level of Equanimity increases during college also report greater-than-average growth in their ability to get along with other races and cultures. Considering that equanimity involves feeling centered and having a positive outlook on life— qualities that in all likelihood enable one to feel empathetic, interested in, and connected to others—this positive effect is not surprising.

Growth in levels of Religious Engagement is negatively related to the student's commitment to promoting racial understanding. A possible explanation concerns the tendency for many religious groups to be racially homogeneous. If after entering college, a highly religiously engaged student remains highly engaged in the practice of his faith, this could have the effect of isolating that student from students of other faiths (or no faith), thereby limiting opportunities for interracial interaction. Since interracial interaction has been shown to be a positive factor in strengthening students' interest in racial issues (Chang, Astin, and Kim, 2004), students who are deprived of opportunities for such interaction would be less likely to increase a personal commitment to promoting racial understanding.

A final significant finding concerns Religious Struggle, which proved to have a weak positive relationship to the student's commitment to promoting racial understanding. Once again, we can only speculate as to the reasons for this somewhat unexpected effect. Perhaps the experience of a substantial religious struggle causes some students to be more empathetic with disadvantaged minority groups.

Impact of College Experiences on Outcomes

In the preceding chapters we have identified a number of college experiences and educational practices that facilitate students' spiritual development, and in the next chapter we advocate for greater utilization of some of these practices and experiences by colleges and universities. From the point of view of higher education institutions and their faculty and staff, such advocacy raises a very practical question: if we were to embrace more of the experiences and practices that facilitate students' spiritual development, what will the consequences be for other educational outcomes? To answer this question we shall employ the same eight "traditional" outcomes described earlier in this chapter, and look into our data to see how these outcomes are affected by various student experiences and educational practices.

Intellectual/Academic Outcomes

A number of curricular experiences that were found to promote students' spiritual development also appear to be key to how students perform academically and how they view themselves intellectually. We begin our exploration by looking at our measure of academic performance, the student's grade point average (GPA). Taking *service-learning* courses, for example, has a direct positive effect on students' overall GPA; students who have done community service work as part of a class tend to earn somewhat higher grades during college than do students who have not taken such courses. (This same effect has been demonstrated in other studies and writings on service learning, such as Astin and Sax, 1998; Eyler and Giles, 1999.) For example, among students who earned a B+ average in high school, 46 percent of those who engage in community service as part of a class earn average grades of at least B+ in college, compared to 35 percent of those with no such course experience. Similarly, among students who earned an A− average in high school, 65 percent of those who engage in course-based service during college earn at least a B+ average in college, compared to 57 percent of those who take no service-learning courses. One could argue that students who take service-learning courses tend to major in fields where the grading is "easy." In our multivariate analyses, however, we controlled for any effects of the student's major *before* examining the possible effect of taking service-learning courses (the fields of education, fine arts, mathematics, and health professions turned out to award higher-than-average grades, while engineering tended to award lower-than-average grades). One might also argue that service-learning courses award higher grades than other types of courses, but it is doubtful whether many students take enough such courses to substantially affect their cumulative GPAs.

Study abroad is another curricular experience that positively affects the student's academic performance. Students who spend some time studying abroad get better overall grades and are also more likely to aspire to higher degrees than are comparable students who do not experience study abroad. These findings are also confirmed by other investigators (Carlson et al., 1990; Ryan and Twibell, 2000).

As would be expected, GPA is substantially impacted by *hours spent studying*, as is the student's interest in pursuing an advanced degree. In fact, most of the experiences that enhance GPA also strengthen the student's interest in postgraduate work. These two outcomes are closely linked, of course, given that most graduate and professional schools rely heavily on the student's undergraduate GPA in their admissions process.

Exposure to *interdisciplinary courses,* which usually address complex topics such as global sustainability or urban renewal from the perspective of two or more disciplines, enhances all three of the students' intellectual/academic outcomes: grades, educational aspirations, and intellectual self-esteem. As other researchers have also determined, interdisciplinary courses have the power to engage students intellectually, to expand their thinking, and to motivate them academically (Field, Lee, and Field, 1994).

Working while in college is very much a central experience in the life of today's college student; our results present a somewhat mixed picture as far as effects on intellectual/academic outcomes are concerned. Several questions in the survey explored different aspects of work, including full-time work, part-time work on campus, and part-time work off campus. Eleven percent of students tell us that they worked full time while they were attending college, while 69 percent report that they had worked part time in a typical week during the past academic year. Forty-nine percent performed part-time work on campus, and 53 percent worked part time, off campus. A majority of students thus combine some form of work with their academic studies in order to cover at least part of their educational costs.

Not surprisingly, students who work full time do less well academically as reflected in the grades they receive, although part-time work appears to contribute to students' intellectual/academic outcomes. (Full-time work also impairs the student's ability to complete a program of study; see Astin, 2005.) The nature of the benefits from part-time work, however, varies depending on whether students work on or off campus: working part time on campus seems to enable students to perform better academically, while working part time off campus appears to increase students' motivation for further education. Since working off campus exposes students to the employment sector, including many kinds of semi-skilled jobs, such experience may well motivate them to pursue further education to enhance their future employment prospects.

Part-time work on campus may benefit students academically because it provides opportunities to learn more about the intricacies of campus life and the role of various offices and campus facilities. Developing networks can also facilitate academic work, since getting to know staff or faculty personally can provide students with opportunities to receive personal advice about courses or services on campus. The proximity of on-campus work to students' academic life can also play a role in managing time, since it allows students to spend less time getting to and from work.

Several other "spiritually related" activities and behaviors also show a direct positive impact on academic performance and intellectual development. In addition to service learning, that is, service that is directly linked to a course, other activities also involve students in extending themselves on behalf of others—activities such as *volunteer work* (outside of service learning) and *charitable giving*—that directly relate to how students develop academically. Donating money to charity also enhances the development of intellectual self-esteem: the number of high-scorers on intellectual self-esteem increases by 6 percent among students who frequently donate money to charity, while those who never donate money show a decline of 2 percent in high-scorers during the college years. These results, when viewed in the light of findings reported in Chapters Four and Five, suggest that enabling students to become more *other-directed* can be of significant benefit, not just to their spiritual development but to their holistic development as well.

We are persuaded that the positive impact of study abroad on GPA and on degree aspirations provides still another reason to embrace programs and practices that encourage students to consider the "other," to develop an understanding of differences and of how the self and others are interconnected. We will return to this point again when we examine students' personal development with respect to diversity concerns. Finally, the fact that *self-reflection* shows a direct positive effect on intellectual self-esteem further supports the importance of cultivating in students a greater awareness of self and the world around them.

A number of experiences and activities besides full-time work appear to have negative consequences for students' academic performance and development. Not surprisingly, engaging in frequent *partying* while in college tends to lower students' GPAs, as does frequently playing *video games* or watching a lot of *television*. Others have reported similar negative effects of these activities on academic performance (Arafat et al., 1974). And, as we report in earlier chapters, these same activities have negative consequences for students' spiritual development as reflected in qualities such as equanimity and ethic of caring (see Chapters Four and Five).

Being a member of a *sorority or fraternity* also shows negative consequences for students' grades. For example, there is a net decline of 23 percent between high school and college in the number of students overall earning average grades of B+ or better. However, among students who join fraternities or sororities, the net decline is 30 percent, compared to only 22 percent among independent students. Other activities showing a negative effect on college GPA include participating in the Reserve Officer Training Corps (*ROTC*) and spending many hours in time-consuming activities such as *shopping*.

Experiences of a more personal nature yield mixed results with intellectual/academic outcomes. Having a *romantic relationship* while in college, for example, shows positive effects both on students' GPA and on their degree aspirations. The positive effect of a romantic relationship on academic performance is understandable given that it can provide a student with a sense of stability, an overall sense of well-being, and perhaps even a study partner. It also may reduce the extent of a student's partying as a means of finding a partner.

Understandably, having a personal injury or illness is a negative factor for GPA and for intellectual self-esteem. Students will have less time for class and studying as they attend to an injury or illness. In contrast, having a personal injury or illness shows positive effects on the student's aspirations for an advanced degree. Perhaps the recovery period provides an opportunity for reflection about the future, thereby enabling the student to address longer-term concerns about how she might live her life.

PERSONAL/EMOTIONAL OUTCOMES

We turn now to consider how various college experiences and activities affect our three personal/emotional outcomes: psychological well-being, leadership abilities and skills, and satisfaction with college. Only one activity—donating money to charity—shows a positive relationship with all three of these outcomes. As we shall see shortly, the remarkable thing about this particular experience is that it is positively associated with seven of the eight "traditional" outcomes, not to mention most measures of religiousness (Chapters Six and Seven) and all measures of spirituality (Chapters Three–Five). We will have more to say about this in the final chapter.

Positive factors in the development of self-perceived leadership skills include group activities such as membership in student clubs and organizations, volunteer work, participating in extramural sports, study abroad, and full-time work. Such activities necessarily put students in the company of others and provide opportunities for developing interpersonal skills and self-knowledge. Volunteer work can enable students not only to develop greater self-awareness and awareness of others but also to cultivate empathy toward the "other"—all critical leadership qualities. Leadership skills are also enhanced by "inner work," including meditation and self-reflection, as well as faculty use of assigning reflective writing/journaling as a pedagogical strategy. Meditation and self-reflection, of course, can enhance self-awareness. Furthermore, faculty's use of reflective writing/journaling as a pedagogical tool increases students' self-understanding and understanding of others, both key factors in leadership.

Psychological well-being shows weak positive relationships with four diverse experiences that do not appear to follow any consistent pattern: participation in student clubs and organizations, study abroad, donating money to charity, and interacting with faculty outside the classroom. Negative factors in the development of psychological well-being, however, merit some comment. First we have activities that probably contribute to a sense of stress because they make significant demands on the student's time and energies; namely, hours spent studying and doing homework, and having a part-time job on campus. Helping friends with personal problems, another negative factor, could also make significant demands on students' time, but a more likely reason for its negative influence on psychological well-being would be that the student is assuming some of the emotional burden of friends' problems. Finally, and not surprisingly, we find that the student's sense of psychological well-being is also impaired by traumatic personal events, such as a serious injury or personal illness, parental divorce or separation, or the death of a close friend or family member.

Virtually every form of peer interaction positively influences satisfaction with college: participation in student clubs and organizations, extramural sports, group class projects, partying, and even helping friends with personal problems. And, not surprisingly, satisfaction is negatively influenced by the one activity that is most likely to deprive students of interactions with peers: working off campus on a full-time basis. Greater satisfaction with college is also associated with having faculty who engage the student in conversations about purpose and meaning, and who are willing to socialize with students outside of class.

ATTITUDINAL OUTCOMES

A number of experiences have positive effects on our two attitudinal outcomes (commitment to promoting racial understanding, and self-rated growth in ability to get along with people of different races and cultures). Besides donating money to charity, positive effects are also associated with self-reflection and reflective writing/journaling, as well as taking service-learning courses, participating in leadership training, socializing with people of different racial groups, and having faculty who encourage students' spiritual development. It is easy to understand why cross-racial interaction (half of the students tell us that they do so frequently) would reinforce students' sense that they can get along with people of different races and cultures, and strengthen their commitment to helping promote racial understanding. Social contact with people who are different from oneself can often help to forge new friendships and enhance one's understanding of social justice issues. In a similar vein, leadership training and courses that include service as part of the class may have similar effects because they often expose students to people different from themselves.

ROLE OF FACULTY

In considering the implications of these findings for higher education institutions, we naturally turn our thoughts to the critical role played by college faculty. If institutions are to more fully embrace the idea of enhancing students' spiritual development and expand their use of some of the practices that have been found to enhance students' spirituality, significant numbers of faculty members have to buy in. Faculty are powerful role models for students; not only are they the transmitters of knowledge and the facilitators of students' search for understanding, but they are also adults who model behavior that students frequently emulate. Further, there is ample research evidence that the faculty's behavior has a direct effect on students' academic and personal development (Kuh, 1995; Kuh and Hu, 2001; Lamport, 1993).

For all these reasons, we made a point in designing our study to acquire information about the characteristics and behaviors of faculty. In surveying faculty members,[2] we therefore included questions about their own spirituality: Do they consider themselves to be spiritual? What role does spirituality play in their lives? We also wanted to learn how faculty members view the place of spirituality in higher education, whether they think colleges should try to enhance students' spiritual development and facilitate their search for meaning and purpose, or encourage the development of students' self-understanding and values. Faculty members were also queried about their teaching methods and pedagogical style, whether they employ a "student-centered" approach that incorporates practices such as cooperative learning, group projects, and reflective writing.

The results of this exploration show that if faculty consider the enhancement of students' spiritual development to be an important undergraduate goal, or if they practice student-centered pedagogy in their teaching, students tend to perform better academically. Specific practices that promote academic and intellectual development include group projects, service learning, and the use of contemplation. (As mentioned earlier, a growing body of evidence shows that contemplative practices in higher education have positive effects on students' intellectual growth and overall well-being; see Shapiro et al., 2008.) Faculty behavior outside the classroom is also important; students earn better grades and strengthen their aspirations for postgraduate study if they have opportunities to interact with faculty outside of class. Again, these findings confirm earlier research on the effects of student-faculty interaction (Astin, 1993).

Summary

In this chapter we have examined the effects of spiritual and religious development on "traditional" college outcomes such as academic performance, leadership development, satisfaction with college, interest in pursuing graduate study, and ability to get along with other races and cultures. We looked at five representative measures of religious and spiritual development, and sought to determine how growth in the qualities represented by these measures would be likely to affect eight more "traditional" college outcomes. We also explored the question of what the consequences might be, as reflected in these eight more traditional outcomes, if colleges and universities were to begin placing greater emphasis on self-reflection, interdisciplinary studies, and other practices that have been shown in earlier chapters to promote spiritual development. Our major findings indicate that

- During the college years, growth in the qualities of equanimity and global citizenship has positive effects on virtually all of the traditional outcomes.
- Growth in equanimity enhances students' grade point average, leadership skills, psychological well-being, self-rated ability to get along with other races and cultures, and satisfaction with college.
- Growth in global citizenship enhances students' interest in postgraduate study, self-rated ability to get along with other races and cultures, and commitment to promoting racial understanding.
- Growth in spiritual quest enhances the student's intellectual self-esteem but tends to lower the student's satisfaction with college and sense of psychological well-being.
- Growth in religious engagement is associated with a lowering of students' degree aspirations, less satisfaction with college, and a weakened commitment to promoting racial understanding.
- Growth in religious struggle shows a positive effect on students' commitment to promoting racial understanding but negative effects on the students' leadership skills, sense of psychological well-being, and satisfaction with college.
- Students' performance in the academic and intellectual realm is enhanced if their faculty employ "student-centered" pedagogical practices and put a priority on students' personal and spiritual development.
- Educational experiences and practices that promote spiritual development—especially service learning, interdisciplinary

courses, study abroad, self-reflection, and meditation—have uniformly positive effects on traditional college outcomes.

- One activity—donating money to charity—shows significant positive effects on seven of the eight traditional outcomes.

The possible meaning of these findings will be discussed in the next chapter.

CHAPTER NINE

HIGHER EDUCATION AND THE LIFE OF THE SPIRIT

We undertook this study because we saw a large gap in our understanding of how college students develop and a corresponding lack of appreciation on the part of colleges and universities of the need to address that gap. We have chosen to label this gap as the student's "spiritual life." To make clear the distinction between spirituality and religiousness, we have developed separate measures of each; our data show that while religious students are more inclined to be spiritual than nonreligious students are, the two qualities are by no means equivalent. Indeed, they follow divergent paths during the college years, as students' spiritual qualities show significant growth while their degree of religious engagement declines. Our data show that during college this decline is largely confined to attendance at religious services. The sociologist Christian Smith has reported similar findings (Smith and Snell, 2009).

Spirituality, as we have defined it, is a multifaceted quality. It involves an active quest for answers to life's "big questions"; a global worldview that transcends ethnocentrism and egocentrism; a sense of caring and compassion for others coupled with a lifestyle that includes service to others; and a capacity to maintain one's sense of calm and centeredness, especially in times of stress.

Our data show that these spiritual qualities are enhanced when undergraduates are provided with opportunities to experience multiple perspectives and diverse peoples and cultures, opportunities such as interdisciplinary studies, service learning, interracial interaction, student organizations, and study abroad.

Spiritual development is also facilitated when faculty members use "student-centered" approaches in the classroom, when there is frequent faculty-student interaction outside the classroom, and when faculty directly encourage students to explore questions of meaning and purpose or to discuss religious and spiritual matters. And virtually all forms of our measure Charitable Involvement—participation in community service, donating money to charity, and helping friends with personal problems—also promote growth in other spiritual qualities (see below).

Spiritual development is also enhanced by practices that are currently used only infrequently by colleges and universities—self-reflection, meditation, and contemplation—practices that directly encourage students to explore their "inner" lives. We believe that encouraging and enabling more students to engage in such practices could substantially enhance the positive impact of the college experience on students' lives. We explore this subject at length in this chapter.

Spiritual development turns out to be highly compatible with many of the more "traditional" outcomes of higher education such as academic performance, leadership development, self-esteem, satisfaction with college, and motivation for further education. Further, most of the programs and practices that contribute to spiritual development also promote these traditional outcomes.

In our introductory chapter we spoke of why we felt compelled to undertake this study. Over the years, we have been dismayed that higher education has paid so little attention to addressing students' inner lives, in spite of numerous claims made in institutional mission statements about the need to educate the "whole person" and about the importance, not only of developing students' cognitive capacities but also of attending to their emotional development, including their moral and character development. In this concluding chapter, we discuss the more purposeful role we believe higher education potentially can, and should, play in enhancing students' spiritual development.

In considering the implications of our findings for colleges and universities, we must remember that as young adults refine their identities, formulate adult life goals and career paths, and test their emerging sense of independence and interdependence, they often grapple with issues of authenticity, meaning, and purpose. As we have seen through our analyses of students' survey responses and heard through our personal conversations with them, many students are eager to explore the inner dimensions of their lives and to understand what others think, feel, and experience within this realm. Indeed, undergraduates often expect their college experience to facilitate this discovery process. Yet until recently, how college students engage with issues of spirituality and the processes by which they establish and negotiate connections between their "interior" and "exterior" selves are topics that have been conspicuously absent from widespread higher education discourse. Let's take a moment to reflect on why this is the case and to consider how we might do things differently in the future.

Within American society, the spiritual dimension of one's life has traditionally been regarded as intensely personal and private, an innermost component of who one is that lies outside the realm of socially acceptable public discourse or concern. As one faculty member shared in her interview with us, "People are probably scared to reveal their spirituality for fear that they are stepping on people's rights, or not being inclusive." However, in the midst of an era characterized by its "spiritual poverty," there has been a growing societal hunger for what crisis management expert Ian Mitroff and organizational consultant Elizabeth Denton have described as "nonreligious, nondenominational ways" of fostering spirituality (Mitroff and Denton, 1999). In recent years, there has also been increasingly widespread recognition of what seems to be an inherent disconnect between the dominant values of contemporary American society and the perspectives and practices that will enable us to respond effectively, not only to our individual needs but also to local, national, international, and global challenges.

Here we are reminded by scholars such as George Marsden and Arthur Cohen that whereas spiritual aspects of student development were cornerstones of early American college curricula, the Enlightenment ideals, positivistic modes of thinking, and scientific worldviews that began to exert a powerful influence on American thought in the late nineteenth century have continued to dominate societal values and individual goal orientations. One manifestation of the resulting worldview is that rather than providing a developmental context of self-reflection, open dialogue, and thoughtful analysis of alternative perspectives, many of today's college and university environments mirror too closely the strong societal emphasis on individual achievement, competitiveness, materialism, and objective knowing. These orientations, coupled with the post–World War II emphasis on a "business model" approach to education, which emphasizes productivity and cost effectiveness, have resulted in a devaluing of the liberal arts and a shift away from holistic, integrative approaches to teaching and learning toward a more fragmented and disconnected curriculum (Marsden, 1994; Cohen, 1998; Murphy, 2005).

Nevertheless, the broad formative roles that colleges and universities continue to play in our society, combined with their long-term commitment to the ideals of "liberal learning," position them well to respond to the questions of how we can balance the exterior and interior aspects of students' lives more effectively; how we can fully support the development of students' inner qualities so that they might live more meaningful lives and cope with life's inherent uncertainties and discontinuities; and how we can thoroughly and intentionally prepare students to serve their communities, our society, and the world at large. As noted in Chapter One, in recent years growing numbers of educators have been calling for a more holistic education (see, for example, Braskamp, Trautvetter, and Ward, 2006), underscoring the need to connect mind and spirit, and for a return to the true value of liberal education—an education that examines learning and knowledge in relation to an exploration of the self.

PROFESSORIAL PERSPECTIVES AND CURRICULAR EFFORTS

That significant numbers of college and university faculty may be receptive to putting more emphasis on students' inner life is suggested by the results of the national faculty survey that we conducted in 2004–2005. When asked to rate the importance of a number of goals for undergraduate education, 53 percent of faculty members say they consider it an essential or very important goal to "help students develop personal values." And fully 60 percent also consider "enhancing students' self-understanding" as an essential or very important goal. However, only about half as many faculty support a similar focus on students' "spiritual development," underscoring the discomfort many of them feel with the use of the term "spiritual" in connection with higher education. Concerns range from fears about being criticized by colleagues because discussions about spirituality may be perceived as antithetical to academic norms, to the need to maintain a separation between church and state, to feeling a lack of expertise, to worrying that such discussions might be perceived as a form of indoctrination or proselytizing.

As one professor we interviewed reflected: "There are many of my colleagues who would say, 'Look, we are at a university, and what I do is math; what I do is history; and, really, that's my competence. Moving into this other area is not my competence.' I don't feel [my reluctance] comes from a place of, 'I'm not doing that,' you know, like resentment. It comes from a place that, 'This is not my area of expertise.'" In considering how faculty could be better prepared to purposefully engage with students to support their spiritual development, another faculty member told us: "I think some of the resistance in faculty that would have to be overcome is when spirituality gets connected with politicized religion. I think you would have to have some programming on what spirituality really is. What does [it] mean? And how is it connected to religion, and how is it *not* connected to religion? How can you understand it in the most productive way possible, rather than the most problematic way?" We also found in an earlier interview study that the discomfort or uncertainty that some faculty experience in connection with "spirituality" largely dissipates when we suggest that they substitute the phrase, "search for meaning and purpose" (Astin and Astin, 1999).

For a number of years, increasing numbers of college faculty and administrators have been recognizing the importance of offering students opportunities to study abroad, to take interdisciplinary courses, and to engage in course-based experiential field studies (otherwise known as "service learning" courses, designed to engage students in community service as part of an academic course). Our study has shown that all of these curricular experiences can contribute significantly to students' spiritual development. In addition to these academic courses and experiences, higher education has also recognized the importance of cocurricular experiences that are designed to attend to students' "whole" development and prepare them for roles as members of the larger community and the workforce. For example, leadership training, membership in student organizations, community service, and participation in student governance all have long traditions in the student affairs field as programmatic efforts that supplement traditional academic coursework. Such practices have been expanded over the years because of their demonstrated value in preparing students for work and community life. Our study has shown that they can also be viewed as ways to facilitate students' spiritual development.

Before discussing how such educational experiences and practices impact students' spiritual and religious development, let us first briefly review the particular measures of spirituality and religiousness that we developed for use in this study.

WHY SPIRITUALITY MATTERS: A SECOND LOOK

In Chapter One we put forward an a priori case for the importance of spirituality and for why colleges and universities should be making more of an effort to enhance students' spiritual development. We believe that the empirical evidence derived from our study reinforces our case to a considerable degree, especially the evidence summarized in Chapter Eight.

Our study developed and utilized five measures of students' spiritual qualities, measures that were designed to reflect many of the specific traits other scholars have proposed as key elements of "spirituality": Spiritual Quest, Equanimity, Charitable Involvement, Ethic of Caring, and Ecumenical Worldview, in addition to a sixth measure, Global Citizenship, which combines elements of Ethic of Caring and Ecumenical Worldview.

Equanimity may well be the prototypic defining quality of a spiritual person. The scale measures the extent to which the student is able to find meaning in times of hardship, feels at peace or is centered, sees each day as a gift, and feels good about the direction of her life. Undergraduates show significant growth in their capacity for equanimity during the college years, and such growth has positive effects on a wide range of other college student behaviors, abilities, and feelings: grade point average, leadership skills, sense of psychological well-being, self-rated ability to get along with other races and cultures, and satisfaction with college.

Our battery of spiritual measures also included three qualities having to do with one's sense of caring and connectedness to others: Charitable Involvement, Ethic of Caring, and Ecumenical Worldview. Like equanimity, ethic of caring and ecumenical worldview show positive growth during the college years.

Charitable Involvement is a behavioral measure that includes activities such as participating in community service, donating money to charity, and helping friends with personal problems. All three of these activities are associated with positive college outcomes. In particular, donating money to charity is positively associated with growth in most religious and spiritual qualities and with virtually all of the other outcomes of college: better college grades, leadership development, intellectual self-esteem, psychological well-being, commitment to promoting racial understanding, growth in appreciation of other races and cultures, and satisfaction with college.

Ethic of Caring reflects the student's commitment to values such as helping others in difficulty, reducing pain and suffering in the world, promoting racial understanding, trying to change things that are unfair in the world, and making the world a better place. *Ecumenical Worldview* indicates the extent to which the student is interested in different religious traditions, seeks to understand other countries and cultures, feels a strong connection to all humanity, and believes in the goodness of all people, that all life is interconnected, and that love is at the root of all the great religions. While Ethic of Caring addresses "caring" in the sense of a personal commitment to alleviate the suffering of others, students who score high on Ecumenical Worldview see the world as an interconnected whole and feel a personal connection with, and acceptance of, all other beings. We combined these two measures to create another measure called Global Citizenship. Growth in Global Citizenship during college enhances the student's interest in postgraduate study, his ability to get along with other races and cultures, and her commitment to promoting racial understanding.

Spiritual Quest reflects the degree to which the student is actively seeking to become a more self-aware and enlightened person and to find answers to life's mysteries and "big questions." Each of the items that make up this scale includes words such as "finding," "attaining," "seeking," "developing," "searching," or "becoming." Students who begin college with high scores on Spiritual Quest say that a major reason they enrolled in college is to find their life's purpose, and that they expect the college experience to enhance their self-understanding and contribute to their emotional and spiritual development. Although the student's inclination to engage in a spiritual quest also grows during the college years, this is the only spiritual measure that is not uniformly associated with positive college outcomes. Thus, while growth in spiritual questing enhances the student's intellectual self-esteem, it tends to lower her satisfaction with college and her sense of psychological well-being.

Turning to religious qualities, we used five measures in our study: Religious Commitment, Religious Engagement, Religious/Social Conservatism, Religious Skepticism, and Religious Struggle. *Religious Engagement* involves activities such as attendance at religious services, prayer, and reading sacred texts. *Religious Commitment* reflects the degree to which the student finds religion to be personally helpful, gains personal strength by trusting in a higher power, and believes that his religious beliefs play a central role in daily life. *Religious/Social Conservatism* reflects opposition to casual sex and abortion, a belief that people who don't believe in God will be punished, and a commitment to proselytize. *Religious Skepticism* is defined by beliefs such as "the universe arose by chance" and "in the future, science will be able to explain everything" and disbelief in the notion of life after death. *Religious Struggle* includes feeling unsettled about religious matters, disagreeing with family about religious matters, feeling distant from God, and questioning one's religious beliefs.

Both Religious/Social Conservatism and especially Religious Engagement decline during the college years, while Religious Commitment and Religious Skepticism show little change. Declining Religious Engagement is associated with increased intellectual self-esteem, greater satisfaction with college, and strengthened commitment to promoting racial understanding. Students' degree of Religious Struggle tends to increase during college, but the consequences in terms of other college outcomes are mixed: increasing Religious Struggle tends to strengthen students' commitment to promoting racial understanding but has negative effects on leadership skills, sense of psychological well-being, and satisfaction with college.

WHAT PROMOTES SPIRITUAL DEVELOPMENT?

Our data reveal several critical types of experiences that promote students' spiritual development: study abroad, interdisciplinary studies, service learning, philanthropic giving, interracial interaction, leadership training, and contemplative practices.

We found that *study abroad* enhances students' levels of Equanimity, Ethic of Caring, and Ecumenical Worldview. Study abroad has been a widely accepted educational practice for a number of years, an experience that exposes students to an unfamiliar culture and usually to a language other than their native one. Study abroad is designed to help students develop an understanding of and appreciation for other cultures and peoples, broaden their horizons, and recognize the importance of thinking globally and of becoming more world-centric in their outlook by challenging the limited perspectives of nationalism and ethnocentrism. In light of our rapidly developing global community, the development of such qualities in the student has never been a more important goal for colleges and universities.

Interdisciplinarity in the curriculum, which was found to promote charitable involvement and strengthen the student's ecumenical worldview, has also become a valued curricular innovation in many institutions because it helps students to appreciate the subtleties of intellectual problems and to see the value of using the knowledge and methods of multiple disciplines as a means of understanding complex issues and appreciating multiple perspectives. Interdisciplinary courses also help students to connect "new information to their existing knowledge and understanding. They help students develop critical thinking and problem solving skills while promoting reflective judgment by encouraging them to synthesize knowledge and evaluate materials provided by experts" (Lattuca, Voigt, and Faith, 2004).

In our study we found community service performed as part of an academic course—otherwise known as *service learning*—to be a powerful means of enhancing students' spiritual questing, ethic of caring, and ecumenical worldview. (One of the spiritual outcome measures, Charitable Involvement, was not included in these analyses because service learning is one of its components.) By linking community service with academic coursework, service learning offers students an opportunity to test otherwise abstract theory in the "real world" and provides community service with an intellectual underpinning. In the past decade and a half, service learning has been adopted as a pedagogical tool by many institutions and applied to a variety of courses because of its power to help students learn academic course material in greater depth and develop other life skills that are essential to their effective functioning in postcollege work and community life. Service learning appears to work because it enables students to identify and direct their personal goals through an exploration of moral and ethical positions about themselves and their communities, and to relate larger social issues to their own lives. Beyond the empirical findings derived from the current study, a considerable body of evidence demonstrates the efficacy of service learning as a pedagogical technique (Astin et al., 2000; Jacoby and Associates, 1996; McClam et al., 2008). Among other things, this research has shown that reflection is a critical component of a well-designed service-learning course.

Community service or volunteer work that is not course-based also has positive effects on levels of Equanimity, Ethic of Caring, and Ecumenical Worldview, over and above the effects of service learning. Recent research suggests that community service per se can have powerful effects on student development, regardless of whether the service is course-based (Astin and Vogelgesang, 2006).

We found that *philanthropic giving* ("giving money to charity"), another altruistic act, enhances each and every spiritual quality. It also shows positive effects on virtually every traditional measure of academic performance, including GPA, Psychological Well-

Being, Leadership abilities, Satisfaction with college, commitment to promoting racial understanding, and self-rated ability to get along with people of other races and cultures.

Giving money to charity is a seemingly simple act, but it expresses one's caring for others through a sharing of resources, which for many students are surely limited. We believe that such acts of charity often constitute genuine expressions of generosity that can reflect strong feelings of connectedness to others. And while service activities involve a sharing of the student's resources of time and energy, charitable giving constitutes a sharing of financial resources that can sometimes deny the fulfillment of one's personal wants in order to share with others. Such giving takes on special significance in a highly materialistic society such as ours and is especially noteworthy considering the considerable concern about finances expressed by many of today's students.

At this juncture we should point out that the last three student behaviors discussed—service learning, community service, and donating money to charity—are components of one of our spiritual measures, Charitable Involvement. The other major component of that measure, "helping friends with personal problems," also shows positive effects on all of our other measures of students' spiritual development. Clearly, this pattern of results suggests that *one of the surest ways to enhance the spiritual development of undergraduate students is to encourage them to engage in almost any form of charitable or altruistic activity.* In this connection, many of the people who are regarded as "spiritual leaders," people like Mother Teresa and Albert Schweitzer, have devoted their lives to altruistic work. Most religious traditions as well instruct their members to engage in such work as one of the fundamental tenants of the faith.

Another type of experience that positively influences students' spiritual development is *interracial interaction,* which turns out to contribute to students' levels of Equanimity, Ethic of Caring, Ecumenical Worldview, and Charitable Involvement (see Chapters Four and Five for a discussion of these relationships). The most direct ways for colleges and universities to expand opportunities for interracial interaction, of course, are to diversify the student body and to develop relevant courses. Providing such opportunities for discussion of different social views has been found to positively affect cognitive complexity, and the greater interracial interaction that results from such intentional efforts has been found to enhance self-confidence, educational aspirations, cultural awareness, and commitment to racial equity. Moreover, helping students reduce their racial prejudice has in turn been associated with the development of positive values and ethical standards (Antonio, 2004, 2001a, 2001b; Chang et al., 2006).

Leadership training, a common cocurricular practice at most colleges and universities these days, was found to enhance levels of Equanimity, Ethic of Caring, and Charitable Involvement. Campus mission statements frequently speak eloquently of the importance of developing the next generation of leaders, and leadership training in college has been clearly documented as a significant benefit to students. Leadership training teaches students to develop greater self-awareness, develop the capacity to understand others, become more empathetic, and develop the skills of collaboration with others in solving problems and in leading organizational efforts (see Astin and Leland, 1991; Cress et al., 2001; Komives, Lucas, and McMahon, 2006).

CONTEMPLATIVE PRACTICES

So far we have been discussing educational practices that are already being used quite extensively by colleges and universities. There is, however, a set of powerful educational tools that have been employed only sparingly by higher education institutions: contemplative practices such as meditation and self-reflection. Our study found that *contemplative practices are among the most powerful tools at our disposal for enhancing students' spiritual development.* Our data show that meditation promotes growth in all five spiritual qualities and that self-reflection promotes growth in four of the five. Both meditation and self-reflection enhance Leadership development, and self-reflection is associated with enhanced Intellectual Self-Esteem, strengthened commitment to promoting racial understanding, and greater self-rated ability to get along with other races and cultures.

Meditation refers to a family of spiritual/contemplative or psychophysical methods and practices that while considerably diverse in approach, share as a common theme or goal: the discovery of a deeper realm of experience or awareness beyond the ordinary discursive (thinking) mind. Toward this end, while some meditative approaches emphasize concentrating or focusing attention on a particular object such as the breath, a mantra, or a spiritual/religious phrase or symbol, other methods emphasize the resting or relaxing of attention from any particular object or focus (J. A. Astin, personal communication, August 2009).

While some may continue to question whether practices such as meditation and other contemplative disciplines have a place in the academy, we hasten to point out that other recent research on the use of meditation in higher education has demonstrated its positive effects on cognitive performance, releasing stress, and aiding in the development of the whole person, including development of interpersonal skills, emotional balance, and academic skills (Shapiro, Brown, and Astin, forthcoming). Partly because of this growing body of evidence, efforts to increase the use of contemplative techniques in the higher education curriculum and cocurriculum have seen an upswing in recent years.

One of the first systematic efforts to promote contemplative practices was the establishment of the Center for Contemplative Mind in Society, founded in 1997. The center works to integrate contemplative awareness into contemporary life in order to help create a more just, compassionate, reflective, and sustainable society ("Center for Contemplative Mind in Society," n.d.). A subsequent initiative of the center was the founding in 2008 of the Association for Contemplative Mind in Higher Education, which supports the development of contemplative pedagogy, research methodology and epistemology, and publications to help faculty explore such matters. The association has attracted a number of faculty and administrators from around the country, and their work has resulted in the development of courses that utilize contemplative practices. These courses are currently offered at a diverse set of institutions, including Brown University, Bowdoin College, Santa Clara University, City University of New York, the University of North Carolina, the U.S. Military Academy, and many more. The association's website lists these syllabi, including a number of other helpful publications ("Association for the Contemplative Mind in Higher Education," n.d.).

FACULTY INFLUENCE ON SPIRITUAL GROWTH

In addition to the curricular and cocurricular experiences just discussed—study abroad, interdisciplinary courses, service learning, charitable giving, interracial interaction, leadership training, and contemplative practices—we find that the faculty's own behavior and practices can play a significant role in how students change and grow with respect to spiritual qualities.

For example, when faculty directly encourage students to explore questions of meaning and purpose, students become more likely to show positive growth in levels of Spiritual Quest, Equanimity, Ethic of Caring, and Ecumenical Worldview. Likewise, if faculty attend to students' spiritual development by encouraging discussions of religious and spiritual matters, by supporting students' expressions of spirituality, and by acting themselves as spiritual role models, students show more positive growth in the same four spiritual qualities as well as in Charitable Involvement.

Remarkably, many of the faculty we surveyed consider themselves to be spiritual (81% indicate so to "some" or a "great" extent) and to be religious (64%). Also, six in ten faculty indicate that they engage in prayer or meditation to "some" or a "great" extent, and about seven in ten tell us that they seek opportunities to grow spiritually. Moreover, almost half of faculty (47%) consider integrating spirituality in their lives as a "very important" or "essential" goal. As one faculty member we interviewed explained: "It's an important part of life. How can you live life without it? Otherwise, what are you? You might as well be a robot." Another commented, "My spirituality is part of me affirming my humanity."

Although many faculty view the spiritual dimension of their lives as important, we nevertheless observe considerable reluctance within faculty on the place of spirituality in higher education. For example, when asked whether "colleges should be concerned with students' spiritual development," only a minority of faculty (30%) agree, a response that seems inconsistent with the fact that the majority of faculty endorse undergraduate goals such as helping students develop self-understanding, moral character, and personal values. As we have already said, this apparent contradiction may well stem from the discomfort many faculty have with the term "spiritual." One wonders if some of this discomfort would be alleviated if faculty knew how we have attempted to define and measure "spirituality" in the current study and what we have found with respect to students' spiritual development.

In other words, it would be interesting to see how many faculty would embrace the idea of assisting students in their search for meaning and purpose (spiritual quest), in attaining greater equanimity, in being more caring for others (ethic of caring), in participating more actively in charitable activities, and in becoming more conversant with different religious traditions and enlarging their understanding of other countries and cultures (ecumenical worldview). As one faculty member reflected: "I'd say there's very little opportunity [on campus] to talk specifically about spiritual matters. On the other hand, there's a lot of opportunity to talk about some of the principles that come out of that, like compassion; a willingness to help others; finding your own voice; and knowing yourself. The principles that come out of a spiritual orientation can be, and in fact are, integrated into a lot of the academic life. But my impression is that talking about it directly is discouraged."

WHAT IS POSSIBLE?

As the early findings began to emerge from our analyses of students' spiritual development, the idea occurred to us of hosting a National Institute on Spirituality in Higher Education at UCLA. The goals of the institute were to share our findings with participants (participants included faculty and administrators from a sample of ten institutions that represented research universities— public and private—and liberal arts colleges); to hear their perspectives on these matters; and to consider collaboratively with them what efforts should or could be possible in the academy to enhance students' spiritual development. Teams of four academics from each of the ten diverse types of public and private institutions joined with our project staff and several outside consultants to participate in the three-day institute held at UCLA in the fall of 2006. The institute's participants eventually offered a number of recommendations for how their colleges and universities could provide more opportunities for students, faculty, and staff to explore spiritual issues on campus. These included

- Offering opportunities for spiritual reflection and discussion during initiatives such as student orientation and programs targeting students during their first and second years
- Using new-faculty orientation as an opportunity to discuss ways to attend to students' spiritual development in the classroom and beyond
- Creating professional development programs to prepare staff, faculty, and peer leaders to participate in and facilitate discussions on spiritual issues
- Establishing places for reflection and quiet dialogue on campus
- Providing interfaith forums on spirituality and religious diversity
- Developing guiding principles to facilitate conversations on spirituality
- Integrating discussions of spirituality in living and learning communities and residence halls
- Hosting guest speakers and forums to encourage discussion on spirituality
- Incorporating spirituality into campus mission and vision statements

Following the institute, and encouraged by the participants' enthusiasm and interest in these issues, we put out a national call on our project website and in the *Chronicle of Higher Education* asking academic colleagues to share with us brief descriptions of any promising practices they might have undertaken to promote the spiritual development of students. Below, we provide examples of actual practices of institutions from around the country that speak to what is possible in the curriculum, and on campus at large, to address engagement with respect to spiritual matters.

"BIG QUESTIONS" DISCUSSIONS

Carnegie Mellon University has developed a Big Questions (BQ) program, which began in 2007. The initiative involves at least thirty faculty, who in collaboration with staff in residence halls, meet weekly with more than four hundred first-year students in small group discussions around "big questions." These questions engage students in intentional conversations about personal values, morals, and responsibility; obligation for and commitment to the larger society; and respect for and appreciation of the diverse perspectives of others. Among the many topics student groups explore with faculty in the BQ seminars are: the meaning of life, the meaning of love, the role of citizens in a democracy, the concept of honor and personal ethics, and the meaning of academic and professional excellence. Indira Nair, vice provost for education, and Jennifer Church, dean of student affairs, initiated the program. It was designed and coordinated by Patricia Carpenter, professor of psychology, and John Hannon, director of student development.

CONTEMPLATIVE PRACTICES

Considering the demonstrated power of contemplative practices, and their infrequent use in academe, we would like to share several examples of such disciplines in informal and programmatic settings.

We have seen a small but growing number of faculty around the country who are willing to engage their students in some form of contemplative practice; yet, many faculty will argue that they do not have the expertise to introduce meditation and other contemplative disciplines into the curriculum. Perhaps as a beginning effort, institutions might consider creating spaces for students where they can go to meditate or engage in self-reflection. In recent years, a number of institutions have been creating such spaces for students, and the response from students has been very positive.

The University of California at Irvine has announced that it is seeking funding to build a Center for Awareness, Reflection, and Meditation to foster contemplation and self-reflection within a space that is dedicated to communication in an open, respectful manner. And at Florida State University, as part of the Spiritual Life Project, the grounds of the new Wellness Building are being designed and built as a park, to provide quiet, meditative space for students, faculty, and staff. In addition, a room at the Center for Global and Multicultural Engagement has been designated as a meditation room, available to any member of the campus community who seeks a quiet place to reflect, meditate, or pray.

Some faculty, as mentioned earlier, have begun to adopt contemplative techniques as part of their courses. In some classrooms, a faculty member may begin a session by asking students to take a few moments to center themselves by means of meditation, prayer, or simple quietness. Other faculty members are introducing reflective writing or journaling in their courses.

Still other faculty give meditation a more central place in the instructional process. One such example is the "life skills" course offered to undergraduate students at UCLA. The course is designed to explore student development issues that arise during the undergraduate years. It focuses on helping students to learn about themselves and their peers. Issues of identity (who am I?), emotional concern (understanding emotion), and social development (communication and relationships) are key topics explored in the course. In addition to covering these topics, students are exposed to meditation and other relaxation techniques. Once students learn these techniques, they are asked to practice one meditation or relaxation technique at least five times during the week and to keep a weekly log in which they reflect on their personal well-being and any negative thoughts, feelings, and experiences they have encountered. Pam Viele, director of the Division of Student Development at UCLA, and her colleagues designed the course.

A more ambitious example of the use of meditation and contemplation to promote self-awareness is a three-course sequence offered at the University of Redlands in California by Professor Fran Grace. The sequence includes an introduction to meditation, a compassion seminar, and a course, Quest of the Mystic. All three courses integrate contemplative inquiry and meditation. They help students learn how to think about what they know and about self-formation and self-knowledge. This course of study follows the wisdom reflected in a verse by the ancient Persian poet Rumi: "Keep knowing, and the joy inside will eventually open the window and look to see who is there." The University of Redlands has also created a meditation room on campus, where these courses are offered and which can be used by any member of the community.

The faculty member who teaches these courses has also produced a video, "The Semester Within," which describes the history and purpose of the course sequence. Students' thoughtful reflections about their experiences are included in the video. As one student reflects: "Meditation has helped me become conscious! I feel like I spent a lot of years sleepwalking through my existence. Now I am awake" (for further information, see also Grace, 2009).

Two other examples we would like to offer illustrate a more integrated use of contemplative practices in the curriculum. Brown University has developed a contemplative studies initiative as an independent concentration under the leadership of Professor Harold Roth; and Ed Sarath at the University of Michigan has developed a B.A. program in jazz and contemplative studies, which has been offered since 2000 in the Department of Music.

As one examines these more ambitious efforts to develop entire courses of study that make extensive use of contemplative practices, one is reminded of the challenges that were faced in the evolution of other innovative programs, such as women's/feminist studies, ethic studies, environmental studies, and the service-learning movement within higher education, all of which have become well established within the academy. We have found that while many faculty and staff recognize the importance of addressing students' spiritual quest and the need to focus more attention on questions of meaning and purpose, many also feel at a loss as to how to proceed, and many others question their expertise: "That is not what I have been trained to do." "How do I introduce such topics in my course?" "How do I respond to students' questions about their inner struggle and search for answers to existential questions?"

In our search to identify intentional programs designed to assist faculty in engaging students in conversations about spiritual matters, we did not find programs that focused specifically on issues of faculty development. However, we did identify a few institutions that are attempting to engage faculty and staff in conversation and reflection about these matters through the use of retreats, lecture series, and celebrations. One such institution, Edgewood College, in Madison, Wisconsin, took advantage of its work with learning communities to devote one learning community to the exploration of spirituality. Readings, journaling, and small group discussions were some of the pedagogical techniques used in this learning community. A retreat from campus was also organized to examine in depth topics such as how a campus can create a culture where spirituality is recognized, cultivated, and celebrated (see *Spirituality in Higher Education Newsletter*, n.d.).

The University of California at Irvine has taken a multipronged approach with the aim of cultivating an institutional climate that can support and enhance the community's search for, and experience of, a spiritual life. The campus has established the XIV Dalai Lama Scholarship Program, which provides full fees and support for students to design projects that advance compassion, peace, and ethics. The UC Irvine Psychiatry and Spirituality Forum sponsors lectures that explore the role of spirituality in health care delivery. The basic purpose of the forum is to recognize, appreciate, and explore the connection between patients' mental health and their spiritual, religious, philosophical, and moral convictions. Its speaker series is designed to provide students with opportunities to interact with major figures in the realm of spirituality.

CONCLUSION

In recent years most colleges and universities have intensified efforts to provide students with educational experiences that engage them with diverse peoples and cultures through the use of study abroad and foreign language programs, workshops, speakers, and seminars. Institutions have also seen the power of service learning and other forms of civic engagement, and the importance of interdisciplinary coursework in helping students to appreciate the value of multiple perspectives in their attempts to confront the complex social, economic, and political problems of our times. Our study has shown that most of these initiatives are also contributing in significant ways to students' spiritual development.

One form of pedagogy that has so far been employed by very few higher education institutions is contemplative practice, such as meditation and self-reflection. Our data suggest that these practices are among the most powerful tools at our disposal for enhancing students' spiritual development.

Our findings also show that providing students with more opportunities to touch base with their "inner selves" will facilitate growth in their academic and leadership skills, contribute to their intellectual self-esteem and psychological well-being, and enhance their satisfaction with the college experience.

In short, we believe that the findings of this study constitute a powerful argument in support of the proposition that higher education should attend more to students' spiritual development. Assisting more students to grow spiritually will help to create a new generation of young adults who are more caring, more globally aware, and more committed to social justice than previous generations, and who are able to employ greater equanimity in responding to the many stresses and tensions of our rapidly changing technological society.

STUDY METHODOLOGY

PILOT SURVEY METHODOLOGY

With a goal of developing an institutional sample that reflected diversity in type, control, selectivity, and geographical region, between late February and early March 2003 we contacted representatives at approximately 150 colleges and universities via electronic mail to invite their institutions to participate in the study. Our intention was to select roughly equal numbers of institutions within each category of type (university, college), control (public, private nonsectarian, Catholic, other religious), selectivity, and geographical region. Ultimately, 46 schools were able to work within a very tight time frame to secure any necessary institutional approval to participate in the study and to provide us with the updated student contact information that we needed.

At each institution, our goal was to randomly sample an average of 250 third-year students. Participating institutions facilitated our direct mail administration of the survey by providing us with updated (current academic year) local mailing addresses for students who (1) had completed the CIRP (Cooperative Institutional Research Program) survey at that institution as entering freshmen in Fall 2000; (2) were still enrolled as of Spring 2003; *and* (3) had given the Higher Education Research Institute (HERI) permission when they completed the 2000 CIRP to contact them again for research purposes. To determine the number of student names that we would need to send each institution for address updating in order to yield 250 juniors (or "enrolled students") per institution, we calculated each institution's expected six-year retention rate using a formula devised in earlier HERI research (Astin and Oseguera, 2002). As it turned out, this method yielded reasonably close to 250 usable addresses at most institutions. The number of names sent to each institution was then calculated as 250 divided by the estimated proportion retained. In addition to local mailing addresses, 32 of the institutions also provided us with students' e-mail addresses.

In late March 2003, we sent postcards to a total of 12,030 students introducing the study and notifying them that they would receive a questionnaire and more information about the project within the next two weeks. Then, in early April 2003, we mailed each student the four-page questionnaire along with a cover letter explaining the purpose of the study. On the reverse side of this letter was information for students pertaining to their rights as participants in the study.

To explore the comparative effects of differential monetary incentives on response rates, we categorized institutions by type (public university, private university, public college, private nonsectarian college, Catholic college, other religious college) and selectivity (low, medium, high, very high). Within each type/selectivity category, we then randomly assigned individual institutions to one of three monetary incentive groups ($0, $2, $5). To the greatest extent possible, and within the limits of our available resources, we assigned at least one institution of each type and selectivity level to each of the three cash incentive groups. For example, students at one moderately selective public college received a $5 cash incentive while their counterparts at each of two other moderately selective public colleges received a $2 cash incentive and no monetary incentive, respectively. Overall, students at 13 institutions received a $5 cash incentive. Students at 17 institutions received $2, while those at the remaining 18 institutions received no incentive. All incentives were included inside the envelope containing the first survey packets that students received.

Two weeks after the initial questionnaire was mailed, we selected a sample of students to receive an e-mail reminder from the total population of students for whom we had e-mail addresses. Two weeks later, a second questionnaire (without monetary incentives) along with a modified cover letter and information sheet was mailed to nonrespondents; one week later we sent a second e-mail reminder to a selected group of nonrespondents for whom we had valid e-mail addresses.

Of the 11,547 students in the sample pool whose survey envelopes were not returned as undeliverable, we ultimately received usable questionnaires from 3,680 students, representing a 32 percent overall response rate. (One institution had to be dropped from the sample because of an inexplicably low response rate.) Women were about 50 percent more likely than men were to respond, and there was considerable variation in the overall response rates for men and women who received different monetary incentives. Money did have a substantial effect: $2 increased the rate of response by about half, and $5 increased it by more than two-thirds. There were positive (but smaller) effects of e-mail reminders. In absolute terms, students who received reminder e-mails were about 4 percent more inclined to respond than their peers who did not receive reminder e-mails (33.5% vs. 29.4%, respectively).

LONGITUDINAL (2004–2007) SURVEY PROCEDURES

In 2004, a special six-page expanded version of the annual Cooperative Institutional Research Program (CIRP) Freshman Survey that is conducted annually by UCLA's Higher Education Research Institute was administered to 112,232 entering first-year students from 236 baccalaureate colleges and universities nationwide. The regular annual survey is a four-page questionnaire including questions about students' backgrounds, high school experiences, expectations about college (including majors and careers), and attitudes about social issues. In addition to the regular four-page freshman survey, the instrument included a two-page addendum containing 160 specially designed questions that pertained directly to students' perspectives and practices with respect to spirituality and religion. Most of the questions in this addendum were taken from the 2003 pilot survey. This addendum is known as the College Students Beliefs and Values (CSBV) Survey.

In Spring 2007, 14,527 students who were completing their junior year at 136 of these institutions participated in a follow-up survey that repeated most of the 160 questions contained in the CSBV Survey addendum to the 2004 CIRP Survey, thus enabling us to measure *change* in students' spiritual and religious qualities during college. This sample of respondents includes sizable numbers of students from most religious denominations and racial/ethnic groups, and their colleges represent all types of public, private nonsectarian, and private religiously affiliated institutions (mostly Roman Catholic, mainline Protestant, and Evangelical). A complex weighting scheme (below) allows us to estimate how the entire population of juniors attending baccalaureate institutions would have responded to the survey.

Since the 2007 CSBV Survey was created as a follow-up to the 2004 CIRP/CSBV Survey, it was particularly important to posttest key items from the 2004 survey, including those that were used to construct the ten factor scales measuring different aspects of spirituality and religiousness. To understand how students' undergraduate experiences may impact their spiritual development, questions concerning college activities, classroom teaching methods, interactions with faculty, discussions on religion and spirituality, and other academic and nonacademic experiences, as well as satisfaction with college, were added to the follow-up survey. As they have during earlier data collection efforts in association with this research, members of the project's Technical Advisory Panel provided valuable feedback during the survey design process. The Spring 2007 follow-up questionnaire was four pages in length, including 150 items having to do with spirituality and/or religion, 59 items covering students' activities and achievements since entering college, and posttests on selected items from the 2004 regular four-page freshman questionnaire, such as student's degree aspirations and political orientation.

SELECTION OF INSTITUTIONS

We invited 77 of the 236 institutions that had administered the expanded six-page freshman survey in Fall 2004 to participate free of cost in the Spring 2007 follow-up survey. These institutions were mainly universities and public institutions. Also invited were

TABLE A.1.   Institutional Participation in the Longitudinal
Follow-up Survey

	Number of Invited Institutions	Number in Survey Sample	Number in Sample for Analysis
HERI pays all	77	63	56
Campus pays some	80	61	56
Campus pays all	79	24	24
Totals	236	148	136

an additional 80 institutions for whom we offered to cover the costs of surveying up to 300 students. These institutions could also choose to survey additional students, but at their cost. Finally, we invited the remaining 79 institutions to participate if they were willing to bear the entire cost of the survey (most of these were religiously affiliated institutions for which we already had sufficient numbers among the institutions for which we were paying all or part of the costs). We grouped the original 236 institutions into the three "pay" status categories based primarily on institutional type. Table A.1 lists for each paying category the number of institutions invited, number of institutions in the mail-out survey sample, and number of institutions in the final sample. A total of 148 institutions eventually participated, but twelve of these were dropped from the respondent sample because they had response rates of less than 25 percent. Thus, the final sample retained for the longitudinal study consisted of 136 institutions.

Once campuses agreed to participate in the 2007 CSBV Survey, they were sent an institutional name-and-address file of their students who had participated in the freshman survey in 2004, and they were asked to update the list with students' current and/or local address and e-mail address.

At the end of March 2007, each of 43,761 students was sent a postcard reminding them of their earlier participation in the 2004 CIRP/CSBV Survey, and alerting them that a follow-up survey packet would be arriving in the mail shortly. The majority of survey packets were sent to students in early April. The packet contained a letter introducing the survey, a copy of the survey questionnaire, and a web link where students could respond to the survey online if they wished to do so. A stamped return envelope was also included as well as a cash incentive. Students from campuses that covered their own costs for the survey received $2, and all other students received $5. (Students at two institutions did not receive any cash incentive because their institutions chose to administer the survey entirely via e-mail.) At the end of April a second wave of survey packets was sent to students who had not yet responded. These packets included a revised cover letter and a second paper copy of the survey, but no additional cash incentive. Students were also provided again with a link to the online survey. Several e-mail reminders that were also sent to students throughout the course of the survey administration proved to be highly effective in boosting response rates. Due to a delay in obtaining updated mailing addresses at four campuses, approximately 2,500 students were not sent the first survey until the end of April. While these students did not receive a second mailing of the questionnaire, those with e-mail addresses received electronic reminder correspondences urging them to respond to the survey electronically.

From the original sample of 43,761 potential CSBV follow-up participants, 3,282 students with undeliverable mailing addresses (including those few who had been followed up only via e-mail but had faulty e-mail addresses) were deleted from the sample. Additionally, 3,650 students from 12 schools were eliminated from the sample due to systematic errors in their addresses or because the institutions had response rates of less than 25 percent. Finally, 126 students who had unusable responses also were deleted, leaving 36,703 eligible participants who were asked to complete the follow-up survey. The final sample that responded to the 2007 follow-up included 14,527 respondents from 136 institutions, reflecting an overall response rate of 40 percent.

Institutions that paid the full cost of participation had a higher response rate (40.3%) than did institutions that were partially or wholly subsidized by project funds (39.7%). At first glance this appears to be an anomalous finding given that students at subsidized institutions received a $5 incentive, compared to the $2 incentive offered at the "pay all" institutions. (The pilot project showed that the $5 incentive increases the response rate by about 6% over the $2 incentive; see Szelényi, Bryant, and Lindholm, 2005.) There are several possible explanations for these results. First, given their investment of institutional funds, many of the "pay all" schools may have actively encouraged their students to respond to the survey. Also, since many of these institutions were religiously affiliated, their students may have been more inclined than students in the general sample to fill out a survey on spirituality. It should also be noted that the "pay all" group received their packets 5–7 days earlier than the subsidized group. Finally, as mentioned, approximately 2,500 students in the subsidized incentive group received only one survey packet at the end of April with no second-wave administration. Since we received their mailing addresses late, these students were not sent the same number of e-mail reminders that were sent to other students, nor did they receive the earlier postcard alerting them that the survey packet was being mailed. Not surprisingly, this group had a response rate of only 15.5 percent.

WEIGHTING

Institutions were stratified into 13 different "cells" representing various types of campuses, as follows. The first level of stratification created six cells: public universities, public four-year colleges, private-nonsectarian, Roman Catholic, Evangelical, or "other" religious affiliation (primarily mainstream Protestant). The private-nonsectarian institutions were further stratified into four selectivity levels: very high, high, medium, or low SAT composite score of all entering freshmen. The Catholic and "other" religious institutions were further stratified into three selectivity levels: high, medium, and low. (Public universities, public colleges, and Evangelical colleges were not similarly stratified because each of these groups was relatively homogeneous in selectivity.)

The "population" in each cell was defined as the total number of first-time, full-time 2004 freshmen in each cell who were still enrolled in Spring 2007. To estimate these numbers we calculated each institution's expected retention rate using a formula devised by Astin and Oseguera (2002). An overall expected retention rate was then calculated separately for each stratification cell by averaging the expected retention rates for participating institutions in that cell. These proportions were then multiplied by the total number of first-time, full-time Fall 2004 freshmen entering institutions in each stratification cell, yielding an estimate of the total number of 2004 freshmen in each cell who were still enrolled in Spring 2007.

The respondents' answers were weighted to reduce the effects of response bias. Because we had extensive personal information from the 2004 freshman survey available on each respondent and nonrespondent, we were able to devise a correction for response bias. Using "response vs. nonresponse" as a dependent variable, we conducted a stepwise multiple regression analysis using all of the freshman questionnaire responses as independent variables.[1] We then used the resulting formula to calculate the weighted regression composite ($\hat{Y}$) for each respondent, which is basically an estimate of each student's probability of responding. We then took the reciprocal of the $\hat{Y}$ as the correction weight. In effect, this correction gives greater weight to those respondents who most resemble nonrespondents in their freshman characteristics. The sum of these weights is equivalent to the number of questionnaires mailed out.

Respondents were sorted into their respective stratification cells and the weights further adjusted so that the sum of the respondent weights in any given cell equaled the total population of students in that cell (in effect, this correction adjusts for the differential sampling of students from different types of institutions). These weighting procedures—both regression to correct for the response bias, and stratification to correct for differential sampling of students by type of institution—were conducted separately for men and women.

The final adjustment involved multiplying each weight by a constant, such that the sum of the weights equaled the total number of actual cases (14,527). This final adjustment was deemed to be necessary in order that the tests of statistical significance would not be biased through the use of a greatly inflated sample size.

LONGITUDINAL ANALYSES

For purposes of estimating the effects of various college experiences on the students' spiritual and religious development during the first three years of college (2004–07), we used a special form of blocked, stepwise linear regression described by Astin (1991), as well as a technique known as hierarchical linear modeling (HLM) (Bryk and Raudenbush, 1992). As shown in a recent study (Astin and Denson, 2009), HLM yields more conservative tests of the significance of institutional-level effects. Therefore, for each regression analysis where institutional-level variables entered the analysis, we re-ran it using HLM to confirm that the effects were statistically significant. There were ten regressions, one each for the ten spiritual and religious measures, which served as dependent variables. The basic rationale underlying this methodology is to estimate the effects of particular college experiences (for example, being a member of a campus religious organization) on a given dependent variable (such as Religious Commitment). In understanding this approach, it is useful to conceive of two types of independent variables: college experiences that could conceivably influence the dependent variable, and "control" variables that might bias our attempts to assess the impact of college experiences on the dependent variable. Since control variables can influence both the dependent variable and the particular college experience(s) to which the student is exposed, the effects of control variables should first be taken into account before the possible effect of college experiences on the dependent variable can be assessed. The most important control variable, of course, is the student's entering-freshman (pretest) score on the dependent variable. And given that there are a variety of other possible control variables (such as gender, race, socioeconomic status, precollege attitudes, values, pretests on college experience variables) that could influence both the dependent variable as well as the particular college experiences to which the student is exposed, it is useful to control as many of these potentially biasing variables as is practically feasible, given the constraints of available data and sample size. For this reason, we used some forty to fifty control variables in each stepwise regression. Please see the note for more technical discussion of the statistical methods we used.[2]

For each of the ten regressions, the independent variables were organized into five "blocks" according to their presumed temporal order of occurrence. Variables within each block were entered into the regression in a stepwise fashion according to how much they reduced the residual sum of squares in the dependent variable. Given the large number of variables, to minimize Type I errors a very stringent confidence level of .001 was used to enter any variable. At the point where no additional variable within a given block was capable of producing a reduction in the residual sum of squares of at least $p = .001$, the program proceeded to the next block. Since the 2004 freshman pretest on the dependent variable was always the first variable to enter the regression equation, it is useful to think of these ten regressions as an effort to identify factors that explain *changes* in the ten spiritual and religious qualities during the first three years of college. The list of variables described here is not exhaustive, but it does cover most of the variables included in each block.

In addition to the 2004 freshman pretest on the dependent variable, block 1—the "control" variables—included a wide range of precollege student characteristics as assessed through the CIRP four-page freshman questionnaire and the two-page CSBV addendum administered at the time the student matriculated as an entering freshman in the fall of 2004. These included academic performance (GPA) during high school; degree aspirations; SAT/ACT scores; the student's gender and racial background; religious affiliation; parental education and income; a number of relevant high school activities and experiences; pretests on other spiritual and religious measures; and pretests on college experience variables (for example, hours per week spent studying in high school would be the pretest for hours per week spent studying in college). Nominal variables such as race and religious affiliation were scored as "dummy" variables.

Block 2 included students' majors in college and their living arrangements while in college (campus residence hall, at home with parents, and so on).

Block 3 included institutional characteristics (type of college attended, size, and so on), faculty characteristics (obtained by aggregating and averaging faculty responses to selected items from the faculty survey), and student peer group measures obtained by aggregating responses of all 2004 entering freshmen (not just those in our longitudinal sample) to selected items from the 2004 freshman survey (these peer group measures also included mean freshman scores on several of the measures of spirituality and religiousness).

Block 4 included students' experiences with faculty practices in and out of the classroom, including their pedagogical practices. It also included student activities such as partying, studying, working for pay, volunteering, being a member of a sorority or fraternity, and participation in athletics and student government as well as curricular and cocurricular experiences, such as study abroad, taking interdisciplinary courses, performing community service as part of a course, and experiences in leadership training. This block also included personal experiences, such as divorce or separation of parents, death of a close friend or family member, and personal injury or illness.

The last block (block 5) included experiences of a spiritual or religious nature, such as having gone on a religious mission trip, being a member of a religious organization, having taken a religious studies class, having done reading of a religious/spiritual nature, and having engaged in self-reflection, meditation, or yoga.

Note that the occurrence of variables in any given block (and of variables in earlier blocks, if any) is presumed to be temporally antecedent to the occurrence of variables in subsequent blocks. Thus, since the student's gender, race, family background, secondary school achievements, and spiritual qualities at the time of initial enrollment in college (block 1) occur *prior* to the student's exposure to residential living (block 2), peer group characteristics (block 3), and particular college experiences, such as service learning (block 4), these block 1 variables could well affect where the student decides to live during the freshman year, what kind of peer group he or she ends up being exposed to, and whether the student ends up participating in activities such as service learning. Accordingly, to minimize the biasing effect of self-selection, these block 1 variables first need to be controlled before the possible effect of variables in subsequent blocks is examined.

What we have described here is actually a form of "path analysis," where the "direct" and "indirect" effects of each independent variable can be assessed by tracking changes in the coefficients associated with each variable through each step in the analysis. A direct effect of any variable is indicated by the fact that its coefficient remains significant even after all other variables have been controlled. An indirect (mediated) effect is indicated when the entry of a new variable into the equation reduces the size of the coefficient associated with a variable that has entered previously. An example of such a mediated effect is discussed in Chapter Six, where the positive effect of attending an Evangelical college on the individual student's level of Religious Engagement can be explained by the very high level of Religious Engagement evidenced by the student peer groups at such institutions.

An additional set of regressions was run in which selected spiritual or religious measures were used as independent variables. The purpose of these analyses was to assess how *changes* in spiritual or religious qualities during the college years affect other aspects of the student's academic and personal development (see Chapter Eight). For this purpose each regression used *residual* changes in five religious/spiritual measures as *independent* variables: Spiritual Quest, Equanimity, Religious Engagement, Religious Struggle, and Global Citizenship. The dependent variable in each regression consisted of measures such as college GPA, psychological well-being, and satisfaction with college (see Chapter Eight). It should be acknowledged that such analyses necessarily yield results concerning the "effect" of changes in spiritual/religious variables that are subject to alternative interpretations. That is, since the posttests on the spiritual/religious measures were obtained at the same time the dependent variable was assessed (in the 2007 follow-up survey), it is at least theoretically possible that the causation could be working in the opposite direction, that is, that 2004–07 changes in the dependent variable (such as psychological well-being) are affecting 2004–07 changes in the spiritual/religious variable (such as Equanimity) rather than the other way around. We have attempted to minimize the chances of this happening by controlling for the effect on the dependent variable, not only of entering-student characteristics but also of all college experiences *before* examining the possible effect of residual changes in spiritual/religious variables. Nevertheless, we believe that these findings, which are reported in Chapter Eight, should be interpreted as suggestive rather than definitive, especially with respect to psychological well-being and leadership skills.

With the single exception of the discussion of the "effect" of Evangelical colleges on Religious Engagement presented in Chapter Six, the text discusses only those variables that actually entered the regression equation ($p < .001$). We have made an effort to mention in our discussions all independent variables that yielded relatively large coefficients or variables that appeared to form patterns, but to avoid further complicating what is already a very complex study, we have not discussed every single finding that was statistically significant.

In a few instances we reanalyzed some of our data employing EQS 6.1 (Bentler and Wu, 2003), a form of "structural equations modeling" (SEM). For example, one central finding (reported in Chapter Six) is that Religious Commitment is positively influenced by Religious Engagement during the undergraduate years. Our regressions had identified several specific religious activities that showed positive effects on Religious Commitment, including prayer, reading sacred texts, attending religious services, and religious singing/chanting (see Chapter Six). Since all of these activities are included in the Religious Engagement scale, we decided to use SEM to test the proposition that Religious Commitment is positively affected by Religious Engagement. The model that we tested thus included four "latent constructs" that were measured by the items making up four of our religiousness measures: Religious Commitment at the time of entry to college in Fall 2004 (the pretest measure on the dependent variable); Religious Engagement at the time of entry to college in Fall 2004 (a control variable); Religious Engagement after three years in college in Spring 2007 (the independent variable); and Religious Commitment after three years of college in Spring 2007 (the dependent variable).

The assumptions related to SEM were evaluated through SPSS and EQS. Missing data were dropped from the final analyses. Although there were no univariate or multivariate outliers, many of the items making up the four measures were univariately skewed ($p < .001$). The Mardia's normalized coefficient ($p < .001$) suggested that the most appropriate method would be maximum likelihood estimation (robust). Despite the fact that the Satorra-Bentler scaled chi-square for the final model was significant ($p < .001$), all other indicators of fit for the model were more than satisfactory. The Bentler-Bonnett's normed fit index (NFI) = 0.854; non-normed fit index (NNFI) = 0.948; comparative fit index (CFI) = 0.951; root mean squared error of approximation (RMSEA) = 0.020; and the ratio of chi-square to degrees of freedom = 1.43. These goodness-of-fit indices suggest that the final model fit the data well.

There was a direct positive effect of Religious Engagement during college on Religious Commitment as assessed in 2007 (standardized coefficient = .84 at $p < .001$). This positive relationship suggests that our original conclusion about the effect of the construct of Religious Engagement is correct, that is, that engaging in religious activities like praying, religious singing/chanting, reading of sacred texts, attending religious services, and so on during college strengthens students' Religious Commitment.

To create a more direct comparison with these EQS results, we used the same four variables in a blocked stepwise analysis that first controlled for the effects of the two entering freshman measures, and then observed the effect of Religious Engagement during college. The resulting partial Beta coefficient of .59 for Religious Engagement was also positive and significant, although considerably smaller than the coefficient produced by EQS. This difference is no doubt attributable to the fact that SEM introduces corrections for attenuation in estimating the effect of latent constructs. We also performed a similar EQS analysis to test another one of our major conclusions, that is, that Charitable Involvement (service learning, helping others in difficulty, donating money to charity, and so on) during college has positive effects on the student's Ethic of Caring and Ecumenical Worldview (see Chapter Five), with similar results.

We add a comment here about "causal" terminology. Whether a particular relationship can be viewed as persuasive evidence of causation is somewhat in the eye of the beholder. For the most part we have chosen to minimize the use of "hedge" terminology, such as "is associated with," not only because it tends to make the text more difficult to read but also because (1) this is a longitudinal study, where many independent variables have been measured prior to the measurement of the dependent variable, and (2) we have been able to control many of these potentially biasing antecedent variables. Even so, readers need to keep in mind that almost any "college experience" variable could, at least in theory, be affected *by* the dependent variable rather than the other way around. This is less true of "factual" variables, such as membership in a campus organization or participation in a study abroad program, than it is in the case of variables that involve judgment, such as whether the faculty "encouraged" the student to do certain things. The most problematic relationships are those that use selected spiritual/religious measures as *independent* variables (see Chapter Eight).

Given that correlational studies such as this can never really prove causation, we have relied heavily on perceived *patterns* of relationships in much of our reporting of results.

TECHNICAL DETAILS ON FINDINGS REPORTED IN THE MAIN TEXT

Since we have attempted to make the main text as "reader friendly" as possible, we are including most methodological and technical detail in this Appendix. As a result, the findings reported in Chapters Three–Nine are not couched in the usual scholarly journal language that we would use if we were communicating primarily with professional colleagues. Furthermore, when we speak of the relationships between our independent and dependent variables, we have avoided the use of technical terms and phrases such as "partial Beta coefficients," "standard deviation units," "effect size," "variance accounted for," and the like. Instead, when we want to convey to the reader some sense of the magnitude of the relationship between an independent variable, such as faculty encouragement to explore questions of meaning and purpose, and one of our dependent variables, such as Ecumenical Worldview, we have done two things. First, instead of reporting actual scores on any dependent variable (such as Ecumenical Worldview), which are completely arbitrary and would have no meaning to the reader, we have defined what we call high-scorers by specifying, a priori, particular patterns of answers to items from the Ecumenical Worldview scale that a student would have to give to qualify as a high-scorer on Ecumenical Worldview. (For details see the section "Defining High and Low Scores" below.) Second, rather than reporting changes in mean scores between 2004 and 2007, we report increases or decreases in the number of high-scorers. (Readers who may be interested in 2004–07 changes in the means and standard deviations of our ten measures can find these data in Astin, Astin, and Lindholm, in press.)

Thus, in Chapter Five we report that students whose professors frequently encourage them to discuss issues of meaning and purpose show a 10 percent increase in the number of high-scorers on Ecumenical Worldview, compared to no increase among students whose professors never give such encouragement. (Those whose professors occasionally give such encouragement fall in between, at an increase of 7%.) While this "comparative percentage increase in high-scorers" approach to a certain extent simplifies what is in fact a much more complex analysis involving many more control variables, it does take into account the most important control variable—the 2004 pretest on the dependent variable—which typically accounts for much more variance in the dependent variable than do all of the other independent variables combined (see Table A.2). Further, we have used this simplified method of quantifying independent variable effects only in cases where the final regression solution clearly shows an independent effect of the independent variable. In other words, we are reporting independent variable effects only when the variable actually enters the equation and remains significant. Readers who may be interested in the actual partial regression coefficients associated with each of the independent variables should consult Table A.3.

Tables A.2, A.3, and A.4 are provided for readers who desire more technical detail about the multivariate analyses. Table A.2 summarizes the ten regressions in which the five spiritual and five religious measures served as dependent variables. Note that with the exception of Religious Struggle, the independent variables account for close to half of the variance in the dependent variables and, in the case of the four other religious variables, two-thirds to three-fourths of the variance.

TABLE A.2. MULTIPLE CORRELATIONS AT KEY POINTS IN THE BLOCKED REGRESSION ANALYSES

Dependent Variable (2007)		Multiple Correlation After Controlling for ...				
	Simple Correlation	Pretest	Entering-Freshman Characteristics	Residence Majors	Institutional Characteristics	College Experiences (Final)
Spiritual Quest	.51	.51	.56	.57	.57	.67
Equanimity	.44	.44	.52	.53	.53	.62
Charitable Involvement	.45	.45	.55	.57	.58	.69
Ethic of Caring	.52	.52	.56	.58	.58	.67
Ecumenical Worldview	.54	.54	.58	.59	.61	.68
Religious Commitment	.77	.77	.80	.80	.81	.89
Religious Struggle	.42	.42	.49	.50	.52	.57
Religious Engagement	.73	.73	.76	.76	.77	.86
Religious/Social Conservatism	.76	.76	.80	.80	.81	.89
Religious Skepticism	.70	.70	.78	.78	.78	.84

TABLE A.3. ENVIRONMENTAL AND EXPERIENTIAL VARIABLES: PARTIAL BETA COEFFICIENTS AFTER CONTROLLING FOR VARIABLES IN EARLIER BLOCKS

Probable Major and Place of Residence (Block 2 Variables)

Partial Betas After Controlling for Variables in Block 1 (entering-freshman characteristics)

	Spiritual Quest	Equanimity	Charitable Involvement	Ethic of Caring	Ecumenical Worldview	Religious Commitment	Religious Struggle	Religious Engagement	Religious/Social Conservatism	Religious Skepticism
Plan to live at home	−.04	−.04	−.06	−.04						
Major: Agriculture							.03	−.02		
Major: Biological Science			.05	.05						
Major: Business					−.05		−.06		.03	−.05
Major: Education								.03	.02	−.02
Major: Engineering	−.05	−.03	−.12	−.12	−.05	−.02		−.07		
Major: English							.06			

Variable									
Major: Health Professions	.05	.04	−.06							.03
Major: History/Political Science	−.03			.03						
Major: Humanities							.03			
Major: Fine Arts							.03			
Major: Math/Statistics	−.04		−.04	−.03	−.03					
Major: Social Sciences		.07	.08		−.03	.02	−.03			
Major: Other Tech Fields		−.03								
Major: Other Nontech Fields								.04		
Major: Undecided				−.03			−.03			

(Continued)

TABLE A.3. (Continued)

Institutional Characteristics (Block 3 Variables)

Partial Betas After Controlling for Variables in Blocks 1 and 2

	Spiritual Quest	Equanimity	Charitable Involvement	Ethic of Caring	Ecumenical Worldview	Religious Commitment	Religious Struggle	Religious Engagement	Religious/Social Conservatism	Religious Skepticism
Institutional selectivity						.02				-.05
Type: University			-.05	-.06	-.03			-.05	-.04	
Type: Public four-year			-.03	.03	-.04		-.03		.03	.02
Type: Catholic										
Type: Other religious (Protestant)	.03		.06		.03			.04		
Type: Evangelical			.03	.03			.03	.05	.03	
Type: Private nonsectarian					.04		.04			
Faculty focus on spirituality	.06	.03				.02			.05	

Percentage female faculty	−.02							
Student-centered pedagogy mean	.06	.07						
Diversity advocate mean			.06	−.02			−.02	.03
Religious Struggle mean					.05			
Religious Engagement mean	.10		.05		.07	.12		
Political orientation mean (liberal)	−.05			−.03				.04
Live on campus mean			.05					
Religious/Social Conservatism mean							.08	

(Continued)

TABLE A.3. (Continued)

College Experiences (Blocks 4 and 5 Variables)

Partial Betas After Controlling for Variables in Blocks 1, 2, and 3

	Spiritual Quest	Equanimity	Charitable Involvement	Ethic of Caring	Ecumenical Worldview	Religious Commitment	Religious Struggle	Religious Engagement	Religious/Social Conservatism	Religious Skepticism
Faculty encourage search for meaning and purpose	.15	.08		.15	.13					
Faculty encourage religious/spiritual discussion	.16	.10	.13	.17	.17	.08	.14	.14	.06	
Group projects		.09				.04			.04	-.03
Reflective writing/journaling			.10	.11				.04		
Contemplation/meditation			.10							
HPW partying	.08				.06	-.08		-.11	-.14	.05
HPW studying/homework		.10		.09			.04			
HPW student clubs/groups		.10	.26		.03			.05	.05	

HPW watching TV	.04			-.08	-.09	-.07	.02	.03
HPW working for pay			.02	.11	.08	.01		.01
Talked with faculty outside class		.07	.17	.11	.09	.08	.07	
Community service for class	.09		NA	.12	.09			
Socialized with different racial groups		.07	.08	.11	.12			
Took interdisciplinary classes			.08	.10	.12	-.01		
Joined a sorority or fraternity	-.01		.14	.01				
Had part-time job on campus		-.01	.06	-.02	-.02			
Worked part time off campus			.05	.03				
Worked full time during school			.03					
Had a romantic relationship								

(Continued)

Table A.3. (Continued)

College Experiences (Blocks 4 and 5 Variables)

Partial Betas After Controlling for Variables in Blocks 1, 2, and 3

	Spiritual Quest	Equanimity	Charitable Involvement	Ethic of Caring	Ecumenical Worldview	Religious Commitment	Religious Struggle	Religious Engagement	Religious/Social Conservatism	Religious Skepticism
Had a personal illness or injury						.03	.04			
Participated in study abroad	.06			.06	.09		.08		-.03	.03
Participated in leadership training	.08		.19	.16						
Participated in football or basketball	.03			-.02			-.05	.02	.03	-.02
Participated in another intercollegiate sport										
Drank beer/wine/liquor						-.07	.07	-.11	-.11	.05
Parents divorced or separated					-.05					.03

Death of close friend or family			.07				.05			−.03
HPW video or computer games		−.12	−.07			−.04		−.04		
HPW shopping		−.03	.05		−.03			.05	.02	
ROTC						−.02				.03
Student government			.12							
Donated money to charity	.08	.12	NA	.15	.10	.08	.05	.13	.07	−.04
Performed volunteer work		.13	NA	.16	.10			.08		
Helped friends with personal problems	.15	.17	NA	.15	.15	.05	.06	.05		
Went on religious mission trip		.08	.09					.17	.10	
Participated in campus religious organization			.08	.03		.16		.25	.17	−.13
Discussed religion with professors, peers, staff	.23	.23	.23	.20		.18	.13	.30		

(Continued)

TABLE A.3. (Continued)

College Experiences (Blocks 4 and 5 Variables)

Partial Betas After Controlling for Variables in Blocks 1, 2, and 3

	Spiritual Quest	Equanimity	Charitable Involvement	Ethic of Caring	Ecumenical Worldview	Religious Commitment	Religious Struggle	Religious Engagement	Religious/Social Conservatism	Religious Skepticism
Self-reflection	.28	.18		.14	.21	.13	.15	.14		
Meditation	.16	.15	.14	.13	.14	.16	.08	.23	.08	
Yoga					.10	.03		.10	.02	.01
Took religious studies class								.17		-.03
Prayer		.21	.15			.54	-.02		.48	-.45
Religious singing/ chanting						.25			.30	
Reading sacred texts	.11	.19			.07	.32	-.02		.36	-.25
Other reading on religion/ spirituality	.16		.15	.15	.18	.23			.22	

Note: All college type variables are listed (statistically significant partial Beta coefficients [$p < .001$] for those college type variables that did not enter the regression are shown in italics). Partial Beta coefficients for all other variables are shown only if the variable entered at least one of the ten regressions. HPW = hours per week.

TABLE A.4. TRADITIONAL COLLEGE OUTCOMES AS DEPENDENT VARIABLES: FINAL PARTIAL BETA COEFFICIENTS FOR SELECTED 2007 SPIRITUAL/ RELIGIOUS FACTORS, AFTER CONTROLLING FOR VARIABLES IN BLOCKS 1–5

College Outcome	Spiritual/Religious Factor				
	Religious Struggle	Equanimity	Spiritual Quest	Religious Engagement	Global Citizenship
Psychological well-being	-.19	.28	-.08	.03	-.03
Leadership skills	-.06	.21	.05	-.03	.02
Intellectual self-esteem	-.02	.14	.04	-.01	.01
Promoting racial understanding	.03	-.01	.02	-.07	.49
Ability to get along with other races and cultures	.00	.06	.03	-.04	.14
Degree aspirations	.02	-.01	-.01	-.05	.04
Overall satisfaction with college	-.09	.26	-.06	-.06	-.01
College GPA	.02	.07	-.01	-.01	-.01

Note: Italicized coefficients are not significant ($p > .001$).

Table A.3 shows selected standardized partial regression coefficients for all the independent variables (other than entering-freshman characteristics) that entered at least one regression. The variables are organized according to their temporal block (2–5). The coefficient for any given variable is the "Beta in" at the step immediately before the first variable from that variable's block was entered. We could, of course, have provided partial Betas for each step in the analysis, or even included Betas for entering-freshman characteristics (block 1), but we chose not to because of space limitations. The Betas provided here give some sense of the magnitude of the effects of all the key independent variables, after all antecedent variables had been controlled. Readers who are interested in more detail about any of these regressions or about any of the supplementary HLM analyses we performed should contact the authors.

In reporting the partial Betas for the six institutional "type" characteristics, we chose to include all variables, including four that did not enter any regression. The reason for this decision is that many readers might be interested in how our spiritual/religious qualities are affected by the type of college the student attends. Note that just because a type variable doesn't enter a regression does not mean that students are not affected by attending that type of institution. Let us see why.

If another variable from the same block—a peer group characteristic, a faculty characteristic, or another type variable—has a larger "Beta in," it would enter the equation before the type variable, and its entry might diminish the type variable's "Beta in" to nonsignificance. But the empirical fact remains: attending that type of college (in comparison to attending other types) does affect the outcome in question. What we have learned is that that particular "type effect" can be *explained* in terms of the variable whose entry reduced the size of the Beta that was associated with that type variable.

A concrete example of this phenomenon is discussed in Chapter Six, where the positive effect of attending an Evangelical college on the student's Religious Engagement is "explained" in terms of the high level of Religious Engagement of the student peer group at Evangelical colleges. (See the highly significant "Beta in" of .05 for Evangelical colleges and Religious Engagement in Table A.3.) Note that the Evangelical type variable never enters this equation because the peer group measure, which is in the same block, enters first and subsequently reduces the partial Beta for Evangelical college to nonsignificance.

A few of the relationships shown in Table A.3 are not discussed in the text, for one or more of at least three reasons: (1) we chose to minimize complexity in what is already a highly complex study; (2) the observed "effect" did not appear to contribute in any material way to the primary substance of the findings; or (3) the "effect" was either very small in magnitude and/or had no obvious explanation or significance.

Table A.4 shows the final Beta coefficients associated with five spiritual/religious measures in the eight regressions where "traditional" college outcomes served as the dependent variables. These results are summarized and discussed in Chapter Eight.

DEFINING HIGH AND LOW SCORES

Given that raw scores on our ten factor scales have no absolute meaning, it may be useful for certain research and policy purposes to be able to classify students according to their scores (for example, "How many students obtained high scores on Equanimity?" "How much of a net increase in high-scorers did we observe over time?").

Since any student's score on one of our measures of spirituality or religiousness reflects the *degree* to which the student possesses the quality being measured, defining high or low scores is to a certain extent an arbitrary decision. Nevertheless, an effort was made to introduce a certain amount of rationality into such definitions by posing the following question: In order to defend the proposition that someone possesses a "high" (or "low") degree of the particular trait in question, what *pattern* of responses to the entire set of questions would that person have to show? We shall use the quality of Equanimity to illustrate the procedure that was followed in answering such a question for each measure.

Equanimity is defined by five items, all of which happen to have three possible responses (scored 1, 2, or 3). The highest possible score (the highest "degree" of Equanimity) is thus 5×3, or 15, while the lowest possible score is 5×1, or 5. For three of the items, students were asked, "Please indicate the extent to which each of the following describes you," with the following response options: "to a great extent" (score 3), "to some extent" (score 2), and "not at all" (score 1):

Seeing each day, good or bad, as a gift
Being thankful for all that has happened to me
Feeling good about the direction in which my life is headed

To be classified as being high in Equanimity, we decided that the student should respond "to a great extent" to at least two of these items, and at least "to some extent" to the third item. This would generate 8 points on the Equanimity scale (3 + 3 + 2).

The other two items making up the Equanimity scale were preceded by the following instructions: "During the last year, how often have you . . ." with the response options "frequently (score 3), "occasionally" (score 2), and "not at all" (score 1):

Been able to find meaning in times of hardship
Felt at peace/centered

A person possessing a high degree of Equanimity, we felt, would not respond "occasionally" to either of these items. Consequently, we decided that in order to be classified as high on Equanimity, the student should answer "frequently" to both items, which would generate 6 points on the Equanimity scale. Thus, the minimum score required to be classified as a high-scorer on Equanimity would be 8 + 6, or 14. (Note that if a student happened to respond "occasionally" to either of the last two items, then that student would have to respond "to a great extent" on *all three* of the first three items in order to be classified as a high-scorer.)

At the other extreme, we decided that a student with a low degree of Equanimity should answer "not at all" to at least one of the first three items, and no more than "to some extent" on the other two, yielding a maximum of 5 points (1 + 2 + 2). If a student happened to respond "to a great extent" on any of these three items, then that student would have to answer "not at all" to *both* of the other two in order not to exceed 5 points. On the final two items, we decided that a student with a low degree of Equanimity should answer no higher than "occasionally" on both, generating 4 additional points (2 + 2). Answering "frequently" to one of these

FIGURE A.1. EQUANIMITY SCORE

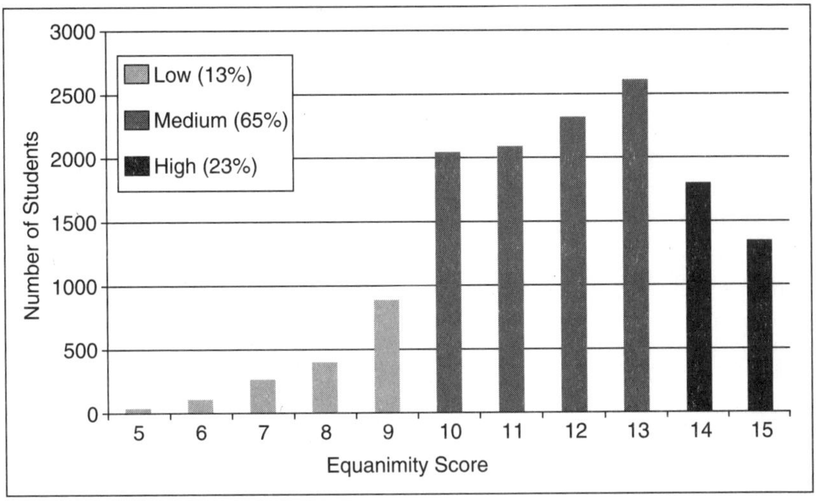

last two items would require a "not at all" response to the other in order not to exceed the total of 4 points. (A similar trade-off in student responses would be possible, of course, between the first three and the last two items.) Thus, the maximum score to qualify as low on Equanimity is 5 + 4, or 9 points. A similar reasoning process was followed in choosing high and low cutting points on each of the nine other measures.

Figure A.1 shows the distribution of scores on Equanimity, which ranges from a low of 5 (students who gave the lowest possible response to all five items) to a high of 15 (students who gave the highest possible response to all five items). Only the two highest possible scores, 14 or 15, qualified as high (black bars), while the five lowest scores, 5 through 9, qualified as low (light grey bars). The bulk of the students, of course, were classified as medium scorers, scoring 10 through 13 on Equanimity (dark grey bars).

ADDITIONAL TABLES

Tables A.5 and A.6 show the survey items making up each of the ten measures of spirituality and religiousness. These two tables also provide statistical details for each measure, including

TABLE A.5. ITEM CONTENT OF FIVE SPIRITUAL MEASURES

	Score Ranges	
	Low	High
Spiritual Quest (Alphas in 2004 and 2007 are .83 and .82)	9–19	26–34
Searching for meaning/purpose in life[i]		
Having discussions about the meaning of life with my friends[i]		
Searching for meaning/purpose in life[h]		
Finding answers to the mysteries of life[a]		
Attaining inner harmony[a]		
Attaining wisdom[a]		
Seeking beauty in my life[a]		
Developing a meaningful philosophy of life[a]		
Becoming a more loving person[a]		
Equanimity (Alphas in 2004 and 2007 are .76 and .72)	5–9	14–15
Been able to find meaning in times of hardship[g]		
Felt at peace/centered[g]		
Feeling good about the direction in which my life is headed[c]		
Being thankful for all that has happened to me[c]		
Self-description[c]: Seeing each day, good or bad, as a gift[c]		
Ethic of Caring (Alphas in 2004 and 2007 are .79 and .82)	8–14	22–31

Item	Items
Trying to change things that are unfair in the world[i]	
Helping others who are in difficulty[a]	
Reducing pain and suffering in the world[a]	
Helping to promote racial understanding[a]	19–27
Becoming involved in programs to clean up the environment[a]	
Becoming a community leader[a]	
Influencing social values[a]	
Influencing the political structure[a]	
Charitable Involvement (Alphas in 2004 and 2007 are .67 and .71)	7–10
Hours spent performing volunteer work[j]	
Participated in community food or clothing drives[g]	
Performed volunteer work[g]	
Donated money to charity[g]	
Performed community service as part of a class[g]	
Helped friends with personal problems[g]	
Participating in a community action program[a]	12–29
Ecumenical Worldview (Alphas in 2004 and 2007 are .72 and .70)[c]	
Having an interest in different religious traditions[c]	
Believing in the goodness of all people[c]	38–45
Feeling a strong connection to all humanity[c]	

(*Continued*)

TABLE A.5. (*Continued*)

	Score Ranges	
	Low	High

Understanding of others[f]

Accepting others as they are[i]

Improving my understanding of other countries and cultures[a]

Improving the human condition[a]

All life is interconnected[b]

Love is at the root of all the great religions[b]

Nonreligious people can lead lives that are just as moral as those of religious believers[b]

We are all spiritual beings[b]

Most people can grow spiritually without being religious[b]

---

[a] 4-point scale: (1) "Not important" to (4) "Essential"

[b] 4-point scale: (1) "Disagree strongly" to (4) "Agree strongly"

[c] 3-point scale: (1) "Not at all" to (3) "To a great extent"

[d] 3-point scale: (1) "Not at all" to (3) "To a great extent" ("Not applicable" recoded as "Not at all")

[e] 2-point scale: (1) "No" or (2) "Yes"

[f] 5-point scale: (1) "Lowest 10%" to (5) "Highest 10%"

[g] 3-point scale: (1) "Not at all" to (3) "Frequently"

[h] 4-point scale: (1) "None" to (4) "All"

[i] 3-point scale: (1) "Not at all" to (3) "To a great extent"

[j] 8-point scale: (1) "None" to (8) "Over 20"

TABLE A.6. ITEM CONTENT OF FIVE RELIGIOUS MEASURES

	Score Ranges	
	Low	High
Religious Commitment (Alphas in 2004 and 2007 are .96 and .97)	12–20	41–47
Seeking to follow religious teachings in my everyday life[a]		
Religiousness[d]		
I find religion to be personally helpful[b]		
I gain spiritual strength by trusting in a Higher Power[b]		
Feeling a sense of connection with God/Higher Power that transcends my personal self[c]		
Felt loved by God[f]		
My spiritual/religious beliefs:		
Are one of the most important things in my life[e]		
Provide me with strength, support, and guidance[e]		
Give meaning/purpose to my life[e]		
Lie behind my whole approach to life[e]		
Have helped me develop my identity[e]		
Help define the goals I set for myself[e]		

(Continued)

TABLE A.6. (Continued)

	Score Ranges	
	Low	High
Religious Struggle (Alphas in 2004 and 2007 are .75 and .77)	7–10	16–21
Feeling unsettled about spiritual and religious matters[c]		
Feeling disillusioned with my religious upbringing[c]		
Struggled to understand evil, suffering, and death[f]		
Felt angry with God[f]		
Questioned [my] religious/spiritual beliefs[f]		
Felt distant from God[f]		
Disagreed with [my] family about religious matters[f]		
Religious Engagement (Alphas in 2004 and 2007 are .87 and .88)	9–13	29–44
Attended a religious service[f]		
Attended a class, workshop, or retreat on matters related to religion/spirituality[f]		
Reading sacred texts[h]		
Religious singing/chanting[h]		
Other reading on religion/spirituality[h]		

Prayer[h]		
Do you pray?[k]		
Prayer/meditation[j]		
Go to church/temple/other house of worship[i]	7–10	20–24
Religious/Social Conservatism (Alphas in 2004 and 2007 are .77 and .81)		
People who don't believe in God will be punished[b]		
If two people really like each other, it's all right for them to have sex even if they've known each other for only a very short time (reverse coded)[b]		
Abortion should be legal (reverse coded)[b]		
Being committed to introducing people to my faith[c]		
Friends share [my] religious/spiritual views[l]		
Conception of God: Father-figure[l]		
Reason for prayer: to receive forgiveness[g]	9–13	23–33
Religious Skepticism (Alphas in 2004 and 2007 are .83 and .86)		
Believing in life after death (reverse coded)[c]		
Conflict; I consider myself to be on the side of science[m]		
The universe arose by chance[b]		
In the future, science will be able to explain everything[b]		

(Continued)

TABLE A.6. (Continued)

	Score Ranges	
	Low	*High*

I have never felt a sense of sacredness[b]

Whether or not there is a Supreme Being doesn't matter to me[b]

What happens in my life is determined by forces larger than myself (reverse coded)[b]

It doesn't matter what I believe as long as I lead a moral life[b]

While science can provide important information about the physical world, only religion can truly explain existence (reverse coded)[b]

[a] 4-point scale: (1) "Not important" to (4) "Essential"
[b] 4-point scale: (1) "Disagree strongly" to (4) "Agree strongly"
[c] 3-point scale: (1) "Not at all" to (3) "To a great extent"
[d] 5-point scale: (1) "Lowest 10%" to (5) "Highest 10%"
[e] 4-point scale: (1) "Disagree strongly" to (4) "Agree strongly"
[f] 3-point scale: (1) "Not at all" to (3) "Frequently"
[g] 3-point scale: (1) "Not at all" to (3) "Frequently"
[h] 6-point scale: (1) "Not at all" to (6) "Daily"
[i] 4-point scale: (1) "None" to (4) "All"
[j] 8-point scale: (1) "None" to (8) "Over 20"
[k] 2-point scale: (1) "No" or (2) "Yes"
[l] 2-point scale: (1) "No" or (2) "Yes"
[m] 2-point scale: (1) "No" or (2) "Yes"

TABLE A.7. CORRELATIONS AMONG SPIRITUAL AND RELIGIOUS MEASURES

2004	2007										
	Spirituality						Religiousness				
	SI	SQ	EQ	CI	EC	EW	RC	RS	RE	R/SC	RSK
SI	(.68)	.55	.48	.34	.39	.48	.78	.25	.72	.61	-.65
SQ	.57	(.52)	.38	.32	.54	.57	.34	.36	.29	.18	-.19
EQ	.55	.43	(.43)	.33	.31	.40	.46	-.02	.41	.34	-.32
CI	.33	.29	.32	(.47)	.51	.39	.27	.15	.32	.21	-.17
EC	.42	.60	.32	.47	(.53)	.61	.28	.24	.22	.17	-.14
EW	.48	.63	.49	.34	.56	(.53)	.32	.24	.22	.12	-.16
RC	.79	.38	.56	.25	.23	.26	(.77)	.08	.81	.80	-.84
RS	.20	.34	.08	.15	.20	.26	.06	(.42)	.11	.03	-.06
RE	.75	.31	.48	.32	.23	.21	.83	.07	(.73)	.80	-.72
R/SC	.63	.20	.43	.19	.12	.04	.80	.04	.80	(.76)	-.79
RSK	-.65	-.20	-.41	-.18	-.09	-.14	-.80	.05	-.72	-.75	(.71)

Note: Intercorrelations above the shaded cells are based on 2007 data; those below the shaded cells are from 2004 (freshman) data. Shaded cells show 2004–2007 (pre-post) correlations.

Key: SI (Spiritual Identification); SQ (Spiritual Quest); EQ (Equanimity); CI (Charitable Involvement); EC (Ethic of Caring); EW (Ecumenical Worldview); RC (Religious Commitment); RS (Religious Struggle); RE (Religious Engagement); R/SC (Religious/Social Conservatism); RSK (Religious Skepticism)

reliability estimates (Cronbach Alpha) as well as dividing points for high and low scores.

Table A.7 shows the intercorrelations for these ten measures as well as for a measure called Spiritual Identification, which we decided not to use in this study because it is highly correlated with measures of religiousness. (Spiritual Identification reflects one's propensity to see oneself and others in "spiritual" terms—twelve of the thirteen items making up this measure include the word "spiritual" or "spirituality." The scale thus reflects the degree to which the student has an interest in spirituality, seeks out opportunities to grow spiritually, believes that we are all spiritual beings, and reports having had "spiritual" experiences.) Note that the upper-right coefficients (above the shaded cells) in Table A.7 are the intercorrelations based on the 2007 follow-up data, while the lower-left coefficients are the intercorrelations based on 2004 freshmen data. The eleven diagonal values, which are the pretest-posttest (2004–07) correlations for each measure, may differ slightly from the simple correlations shown in Table A.2 because of slight differences in the samples caused by the use of "listwise" deletion when the regressions were run.

NOTES

CHAPTER TWO

1. All scales were developed using factor analysis and item analysis. Possible scales—groups of similar items—were identified using principal components analyses with Varimax rotation, following which each potential scale was subjected to an item analysis (Cronbach Alpha) to eliminate items that were not contributing to scale reliability. Considerations of appropriateness of item content were also applied in each stage of scale development. See Note 3 for more detail.

2. John A. Astin (California Pacific Medical Center), Arthur W. Chickering (Goddard College), Peter C. Hill (Biola University), Ellen L. Idler (Emory University), Cynthia S. Johnson (American College Personnel Association), Michael McCullough (University of Miami), William L. (Scotty) McLennan Jr. (Stanford University), Kenneth I. Pargament (Bowling Green State University), and Christian Smith (University of Notre Dame).

3. Our first task was to sort the 175 pilot survey items into broad categories. Initially, we identified six a priori clusters of items that were hypothesized to represent the following constructs: conservative Christian, liberal Christian, "cultural creative" (following Ray and Anderson, 2000), well-being, religious skepticism, and self-perceived spiritual/religious change during college. The remaining large pool of items was separated into two large groups: items having to do with the "interior"—values, beliefs, and perceptions—and items having to do with the "exterior"—behaviors, experiences, and actions. Separate principal components factor analyses with Varimax rotation were performed on each of these eight groups of questionnaire items. Many factor analyses were repeated rotating different numbers of components or with modified item content with the aim of identifying the solution that demonstrated both the best simple structure and the most conceptual coherence. After each analysis, the research team discussed the resulting solution at length, collectively deciding

whether additional analyses were needed. Experimental analyses were sometimes conducted by combining items across the original a priori clusters. Periodically, we also tried oblique rotational solutions. Throughout this factor analytic phase, we would construct trial scales. Once a promising potential scale was identified, a reliability analysis (Cronbach Alpha) was performed in order to eliminate items that were not contributing to scale reliability. The resulting scale was then correlated with other items in the questionnaire in order to (1) identify other possible items that could be added to the scale and (2) explore the scale's construct validity (i.e., does it correlate in expected ways with other items and other scales?). An item that appeared to belong on more than one scale was either omitted or placed on the scale with which it had the highest correlation. Note that in order to avoid any experimental dependence among the scales, no item was used in more than one scale.

4. Beyond such differences in item content and wording, the methods used to develop this battery of measures are unique in several other respects. For example, rather than having all the items that define a particular construct arranged in a single list, the various forms of the CSBV have employed several short lists of items, with each list comprising a set of relatively heterogeneous items (readers can view copies of the survey instruments from the project website: www.spirituality.ucla.edu). While the response mode (e.g., "frequently . . . not at all," "agree strongly . . . disagree strongly") is the same for all items in any given list, it is systematically varied from list to list. As a result, all of our scales are composed of items from two or more of these lists. By contrast, earlier researchers have typically set out to measure a single construct by developing one list containing a relatively homogeneous set of items and asking subjects to respond to each item using a single response mode. We believe that such an approach tends to yield spuriously high reliabilities, especially when the subjects (1) think they have been able to "figure out" what the construct is, and/or (2) strive to give consistent responses from item to item. It should also be pointed out that these ten scales, which were initially developed from the 2003 pilot survey data, were subsequently replicated in two independent surveys conducted in 2004 and 2007. While these three surveys used a similar format—a series of short lists of relatively heterogeneous items—they varied considerably in item content and in the order in which the lists were presented. Moreover, the method of administration also varied: the 2003 pilot survey of college juniors was conducted exclusively by mail (both outgoing and

return); the 2004 freshman survey was conducted at most campuses in small Summer–Fall orientation groups; while the outgoing survey for the spring 2007 follow-up was conducted by mail, with students given the option of either completing the hard copy of the survey and returning it by mail (55% chose this option) or filling it out on the web (45% chose this option). We believe that varying the survey forms and methods of administration in this manner has contributed to the scales' robustness.

CHAPTER FOUR

1. Among college juniors the correlations of Equanimity with other measures of spirituality range from .32 (Ethic of Caring) to .38 (Spiritual Quest); correlations with religiousness measures range from .34 (Religious/Social Conservatism) to .46 (Religious Commitment). See the Appendix.

CHAPTER FIVE

1. Among college juniors, Ethic of Caring is correlated .61 and .51, respectively, with Ecumenical Worldview and Charitable Involvement. The latter two measures are correlated .39 with each other.

CHAPTER SEVEN

1. Religious Skepticism correlates −.84 and −.72, respectively, with Religious Commitment and Religious Engagement.

CHAPTER EIGHT

1. In the survey questionnaire, students were asked to respond to an item where they indicated that they never, occasionally, or frequently felt that their life was "filled with stress and anxiety." To include this item in the measure of psychological well-being, we gave it a reverse scoring.
2. In the 2004–2005 academic year the Higher Education Research Institute surveyed over fifty thousand faculty at more than four hundred institutions, as part of its ongoing Cooperative Institutional Research Program (CIRP).

Appendix

1. Some investigators recommend the use of logistic regression instead of ordinary least squares (OLS) regression when the dependent variable is a dichotomy. However, since an extensive empirical comparison of the two methods using CIRP data (see Dey and Astin, 1993) shows that they yield essentially identical results, we chose to use OLS regression, because the SPSS program includes important options (e.g., "Beta in" for variables not in the equation) not available in the logistic regression program. Further, a recent methodological study shows that OLS regression and logistic regression produce cross-validated results that are essentially identical (see Oseguera and Vogelgesang, 2003).

2. We have performed methodological studies comparing the HLM (hierarchical linear modeling) and OLS (ordinary least squares) regression and found that they yield essentially identical multivariate solutions. Aside from making it easier to examine student-institutional interaction effects (which we are not examining in this study), the main advantage to using HLM over OLS is that HLM provides more conservative estimates of the statistical significance of institutional-level effects, a limitation of OLS that we initially handled through the use of a very stringent p-value (.001) for the entry of independent variables. However, to confirm our OLS findings, we subsequently used HLM to re-run all OLS regressions that produced significant institutional-level effects. Only those effects that were significant ($p < .05$) in both the HLM and OLS analyses are reported here.

   We chose OLS as our principal method because we needed to model our variables in separate blocks according to their temporal ordering. The SPSS program for OLS contains several important options not available in the HLM program. In particular, the SPSS program (1) allows one to conduct path analyses by blocking independent variables in terms of their presumed temporal sequence of occurrence: entering-freshman characteristics, type of college attended, freshman living arrangements (dormitory, private room, with parents), initial major field of study, curricular and cocurricular experiences after entering college; (2) makes it possible to enter the variables in a stepwise fashion *within* any sequential block, a feature that enables the investigator to determine *which* particular variable(s) in the block may be mediating the effect of variables entered from an earlier block; and (3) shows, at each step, for each variable not yet entered into the equation, the "Beta in" statistic, which is the

Beta that variable would be assigned if it were to be entered on the next step.

A currently popular criticism of OLS regression concerns the stepwise feature, which some statisticians object to on a number of theoretical grounds. We have examined these objections and found either that they are erroneous or that they apply equally to any multivariate method, including HLM. For details see Astin and Denson (2009).

REFERENCES

Allport, G. W., and J. M. Ross. Personal religious orientation and pre-judice. *Journal of Personality and Social Psychology*, 5(4) (1967): 432–43

Antonio, A. L. Diversity and the influence of friendship groups in college. *Review of Higher Education*, 25(1) (2001a): 63–89

Antonio, A. L. The role of interracial interaction in the development of leadership skills and cultural knowledge and understanding. *Research in Higher Education*, 42(5) (2001b): 593–617

Antonio, A. L. The influence of friendship groups on intellectual self-confidence and educational aspirations in college. *Journal of Higher Education*, 75(4) (2004): 446–71

Arafat, I. S., J. M. Hulbert, and P. A. Filmer. Academic achievement and television viewing: The case of the college student. Paper delivered at the Annual Meeting of the Southern Sociological Society (1974)

Ash, S. L., and P. H. Clayton. The articulated learning: An approach to guided reflection and assessment. *Innovative Higher Education*, 29(2) (2004): 137–54

Ashmos, D. P., and D. Duchon. Spirituality at work: A conceptualization and measure. *Journal of Management Inquiry*, 9(2) (2000): 134–45

"The Association for the Contemplative Mind in Higher Education," n.d., www.acmhe.org/publications.html (accessed 9/29/09)

Astin, A. W. *Assessment for excellence: The philosophy and practice of assessment and evaluation in higher education.* New York: Macmillan/Oryx (1991)

Astin, A. W. *What matters in college? Four critical years revisited.* San Francisco: Jossey-Bass (1993)

Astin, A. W. The role of service in higher education. *About Campus*, 1(1) (1996): 14–19.

Astin, A. W. Making sense out of degree completion rates. *Journal of College Student Retention*, 7(1) (2005): 5–17

Astin, A. W., and H. S. Astin, with the assistance of A. L. Antonio, J. S. Astin, and C. M. Cress. *Meaning and spirituality in the lives of college*

206 REFERENCES

206 REFERENCES

206 REFERENCES

206 REFERENCES
206 REFERENCES

faculty: A study of values, authenticity, and stress. Higher Education Research Institute, UCLA (1999)

Astin, A. W., H. S. Astin, and J. L. Lindholm. Assessing students' spiritual and religious qualities. *Journal of College Student Development* (in press)

Astin, A. W., and N. Denson. Multi-campus studies of college impact: Which statistical method is appropriate? *Research in Higher Education,* 50(4) (2009): 354–67

Astin, A. W., and J. P. Keen. Equanimity and spirituality. *Religion and Education,* 33(2) (2006): 1–8

Astin, A. W., and L. Oseguera. *Degree attainment rates at American colleges and universities.* Higher Education Research Institute, UCLA (2002)

Astin, A. W., and L. J. Sax. How undergraduates are affected by service participation. *Journal of College Student Development,* 39(3) (1998): 251–63

Astin, A. W., L. J. Sax, and J. Avalos. Long-term effects of volunteerism during the undergraduate years. *Review of Higher Education,* 22(2) (1999): 187–202

Astin, A. W., and L. J. Vogelgesang, with the assistance of K. Misa, J. Anderson, N. Denson, U. Jayakumar, V. Saenz, and E. Yamamura. *Understanding the effects of service learning: A study of students and faculty.* Higher Education Research Institute, UCLA (2006)

Astin, A. W., L. J. Vogelgesang, E. K. Ikeda, and J. A. Yee. *How service learning affects students.* Los Angeles: Higher Education Research Institute, UCLA (2000)

Astin, H. S., and C. Leland. *Women of influence, women of vision: A cross-generational study of leaders and social change.* San Francisco: Jossey-Bass (1991)

Baker, D. C. Studies of the inner life: The impact of spirituality on quality of life. *Quality of Life Research,* 12(Supp. 1) (2003): 51–57

Batson, C. D. Religion as prosocial agent or double agent? *Journal for the Scientific Study of Religion,* 15(1) (1976): 29–45

Beck, C. Education for spirituality. *Interchange,* 17(2) (1986): 148–56

Belenky, M., B. M. Clinchy, N. R. Goldberger, and J. M. Tarule. *Women's ways of knowing: The development of self, voice, and mind.* New York: Basic Books (1986)

Bentler, P. M., and E. J. C. Wu. *EQS 6.1 for Windows: User's Guide.* Encino, CA: Multivariate Software, Incorporated (2003)

Braskamp, L. A., L. C. Trautvetter, and K. Ward. *Putting students first: How colleges develop students purposefully.* Bolton, MA: Anker (2006)

Brinkley, D. G. *The unfinished presidency: Jimmy Carter's journey beyond the White House.* New York: Viking Press (1998)

Bruce, M. A., and D. Cockreham. Enhancing the spiritual development of adolescent girls. *Professional School Counseling, 7*(5) (2004): 334–42

Bryant, A. N. Exploring religious pluralism in higher education: Non-majority religious perspectives among entering first-year college students. *Religion and Education, 33*(1) (2006): 1–25

Bryk, A. S., and S. W. Raudenbush. *Hierarchical linear models: Applications and data analysis methods.* Newbury Park, CA: Sage (1992)

Burack, E. Spirituality in the workplace. *Journal of Organizational Change Management, 12*(4) (1999): 280–91

Cannister, M. W. Enhancing spirituality among college freshmen through faculty mentoring. *Research on Christian Higher Education, 5* (1998): 83–103

Carlson, J. S., B. B. Burn, J. Useem, and D. Yachimowicz. *Study abroad: The experience of American undergraduates.* New York: Greenwood (1990)

"The Center for Contemplative Mind in Society," n.d., www .contemplativemind.org (accessed 9/29/09)

Chang, M. J., A. W. Astin, and D. Kim. Cross-racial interaction among undergraduates: Some consequences, causes, and patterns. *Research in Higher Education, 45*(5) (2004): 529–53

Chang, M. J., N. Denson, V. Saenz, and K. Misa. The educational benefits of cross-racial interaction for undergraduates. *Journal of Higher Education, 77*(3) (2006): 430–55

Chickering, A. W., J. C. Dalton, and L. Stamm. *Encouraging authenticity and spirituality in higher education.* San Francisco: Jossey-Bass (2005)

Cohen, A. M. *The shaping of American higher education: Emergence and growth of the contemporary system.* San Francisco: Jossey-Bass (1998)

Cook, S. W., P. D. Borman, M. A. Moore, and M. A. Kunkel. College students' perceptions of spiritual people and religious people. *Journal of Psychology and Theology, 28*(2) (2000): 125–37

Crawford, E., M. O'Dougherty Wright, and A. S. Masten. Resiliency and spirituality in youth. In E. C. Roehlkepartain, P. E. King, L. Wagener, and P. L. Bensen (Eds.), *The handbook of spiritual development in childhood and adolescence.* Thousand Oaks, CA: Sage (2006): 355–70

Cress, C. M., H. S. Astin, K. Zimmerman-Oster, and J. Burkhardt. Developmental outcomes of college students' involvement in leadership activities. *Journal of College Student Development, 42*(1) (2001): 15–27

Dalai Lama, H. H. *Freedom in exile: The autobiography of the Dalai Lama.* San Francisco: Harper (1991)

Daloz, L. A. P., C. H. Keen, J. P. Keen, and S. D. Parks. *Common fire: Leading lives of commitment in a complex world.* Boston: Beacon Press (1996)

De Souza, M. Contemporary influences on the spirituality of young people: Implications for education. *International Journal of Childhood Spirituality, 8*(3) (2003): 269–79

Dehler, G. E., and M. A. Welsh. Discovering the keys: Spirit in teaching and the journey of learning. *Journal of Management Education, 21*(4) (1997): 496–508

Dey, E. L., and A. W. Astin. Statistical alternatives for studying college student retention: A comparative analyses of logit, probit, and linear regression. *Research in Higher Education, 34*(5) (1993): 569–81

Dyson, J., M. Cobb, and D. Forman. The meaning of spirituality: A literature review. *Journal of Advanced Nursing, 26*(6) (1997): 1183–88

Elkins, D. N., L. J. Hedstrom, L. L. Hughes, J. A. Leaf, and C. Saunders. Toward a humanistic-phenomenological spirituality: Definitions, description, and measurement. *Journal of Humanistic Psychology, 28*(4) (1988): 5–18

Eyler, J., and D. E. Giles. *Where's the learning in service learning?* San Francisco: Jossey-Bass (1999)

Fetzer Institute. *Multidimensional measurement of religiousness/spirituality for use in health research.* Kalamazoo, MI: Fetzer Institute (2003): 1

Field, M., R. Lee, and M. L. Field. Assessing interdisciplinary learning. *New Directions for Teaching and Learning, 58* (1994): 69–84

Fowler, J. W. *Stages of faith: the psychology of human development and the quest for meaning.* New York: Harper Collins (1981)

Frankl, V. E. *Man's search for meaning.* New York: Washington Square Press (1984)

Fuller, R. C. *Spiritual but not religious: Understanding unchurched America.* New York: Oxford Press (2001)

Genia, V. The Spiritual Experience Index: A measure of spiritual maturity. *Journal of Religion and Health, 30*(4) (1991): 337–47

Gibbons, P. Spirituality at work: Definitions, measures, assumptions, and validity claims. In J. Biberman and M. D. Whitty (Eds.), *Work and spirit: A reader of new spiritual paradigms for organizations.* Scranton, PA: University of Scranton Press (2000): 111–31

Giles, D. E., and J. Eyler. The impact of a college community service laboratory on students' personal, social, and cognitive outcomes. *Journal of Adolescence, 17* (1994): 327–39

Gilligan, C. *In a different voice.* Cambridge, MA: Harvard University Press (1982)

Goddard, N. C. A response to Dawson's critical analysis of "spirituality" as integrative energy. *Journal of Advanced Nursing, 31*(4) (2000): 968–79

Grace, F. Pedagogy of reverence: A narrative account. *Religion and Education, 36*(2) (2009)

Hall, T. W., and K. J. Edwards. The Spiritual Assessment Inventory: A theistic model and measure for assessing spiritual development. *Journal for the Scientific Study of Religion, 41*(2) (2002): 341–57

Hatcher, J. A., and R. G. Bringle. Reflection. *College Teaching, 45*(4) (1997): 153–58

Hayes, S. C. Making sense of spirituality. *Behaviorism, 12*(2) (1984): 99–110

Helminiak, D. A. *Spiritual development: An interdisciplinary study.* Chicago: Loyola University Press (1987)

Higher Education Research Institute. *A social change model of leadership development: Guidebook III.* Higher Education Research Institute, UCLA (1996)

Hill, P. C., and R. W. Hood Jr. (Eds.). *Measures of religiosity.* Birmingham, AL: Religious Education Press (1999)

Hill, P. C., and K. I. Pargament. Advances in the conceptualization and measurement of religion and spirituality. *American Psychologist 58*(1) (2003): 64–74

Hill, P. C., K. I. Pargament, R. W. Hood Jr., M. E. McCullough, J. P. Swyers, D. B. Lawson, and B. J. Zinnbauer. Conceptualizing religion and spirituality: Points of commonality, points of departure. *Journal for the Theory of Social Behavior, 30*(1) (2000): 51–77

Hindman, D. M. From splintered lives to whole persons: Facilitating spiritual development of college students. *Religious Education, 97*(2) (2002): 165–82

Hodge, D. R. The intrinsic spirituality scale: A new six-item instrument for assessing the salience of spirituality as a motivational construct. *Journal of Social Sciences Research, 30*(1) (2003): 41–61

Holland, J. L. *Making vocational choices: A theory of vocational personalities and work environments.* Englewood Cliffs, NJ: Prentice Hall (1985)

hooks, b. *All about love: New visions.* New York: William Morrow (2000): 77

Idler, E. Organizational religiousness. In *Multidimensional measurement of religiousness/spirituality for use in health research: A report to the Fetzer Institute/National Institute on Aging Working Group.* Kalamazoo, MI: Fetzer Institute (1999): 75–80

Jacoby, B., and Associates. *Service-learning in higher education: Concepts and practices.* San Francisco: Jossey-Bass (1996)

Johnson, C. V., and J. A. Hayes. Troubled spirits: Prevalence and predictors of religious and spiritual concerns among university students and counseling center clients. *Journal of Counseling Psychology, 50* (2003): 409–19

Josselson, R. *Finding herself: Pathways to identity development in women.* San Francisco: Jossey-Bass (1987)

Kazanjian, V. H., and P. J. Laurence (Eds.). *Education as transformation: Religious pluralism, spirituality, and a new vision for higher education in America.* New York: Peter Lang (2000)

Kegan, R. *The evolving self: method and process in human development.* Cambridge, MA: Harvard University Press (1982)

King, A. S. Spirituality: Transformation and metamorphosis. *Religion, 26*(4) (1996): 343–51

King, C. S. *My life with Martin Luther King, Jr.* (rev. ed.). New York: Henry Holt (1993)

Klaassen, D. W., and M. J. McDonald. Quest and identity development: Reexamining pathways for existential search. *International Journal for the Psychology of Religion, 12*(3) (2002): 189–200

Kohlberg, L. *Essays on moral development, Vol 1: The philosophy of moral development.* New York: Harper & Row (1981)

Komives, S. R., N. Lucas, and T. R. McMahon. *Exploring leadership: For college students who want to make a difference* (2nd ed.). San Francisco: Jossey-Bass (2006)

Korn, J. S. *Another dimension of campus date rape: The college community reaction.* Unpublished doctoral dissertation, University of California, Los Angeles (1996)

Kouzes, J. M., and B. Z. Posner. *The leadership challenge* (3rd ed.). San Francisco: Jossey-Bass (1993)

Krahnke, K., and L. Hoffman. The rise of religion and spirituality in the workplace: Employees' rights and employers' accommodations. *Journal of Behavioral and Applied Management, 3*(3) (2002): 277–87

Kuh, G. D. The other curriculum: Out-of-class experiences associated with student learning and personal development. *Journal of Higher Education, 66*(2) (1995): 123–55

Kuh, G. D., and S. Hu. The effects of student-faculty interaction in the 1990s. *Review of Higher Education, 24*(3) (2001): 309–32

Lamport, M. A. Student-faculty informal interaction and the effect on college student outcomes: A review of the literature. *Adolescence, 28*(112) (1993): 971–90

Lattuca, L. R., L. J. Voigt, and K. Q. Faith. Does interdisciplinarity promote learning? Theoretical support and researchable questions. *Review of Higher Education, 28*(1) (2004): 23–48

Lee, D. M. Reinventing the university: From institutions to communities of higher education. *Journal of Adult Development, 6*(3) (1999): 175–83

Levin, J. Private religious practices. In *Multidimensional measurement of religiousness/spirituality for use in health research: A report to the Fetzer Institute/National Institute on Aging Working Group.* Kalamazoo, MI: Fetzer Institute (1999): 39–42

Lindholm, J. A., and H. S. Astin. Spirituality and pedagogy: Faculty's spirituality and use of student-centered approaches to undergraduate teaching. *Review of Higher Education, 31*(2) (2008): 185–207

Lindholm, J. A., H. S. Astin, and A. W. Astin. *Spirituality and the professoriate: A national study of faculty beliefs, attitudes, and behaviors.* Higher Education Research Institute, UCLA (2005)

Lott, C. E., C. W. Michelmore, M. Sullivan-Cosetti, and J. A. Wister. Learning through service: A faculty perspective. *Liberal Education, 83*(1) (1997): 40–45

Love, P. G., and D. Talbot. Defining spiritual development: A missing consideration for student affairs. *NASPA Journal, 37*(1) (1999): 361–75

MacDonald, D. A. Spirituality: Description, measurement, and relation to the five factor model of personality. *Journal of Personality, 68*(1) (2000): 153–97

Maher, M. F., and T. K. Hunt. Spirituality reconsidered. *Counseling and Values, 38*(1) (1993): 21–28

Mandela, N. *Long walk to freedom: The autobiography of Nelson Mandela.* Boston: Little Brown (1994)

Mann, R. D. *The light of consciousness: Explorations in transpersonal psychology.* Albany, NY: SUNY Press (1984)

Marsden, G. M. *The soul of the American university: From Protestant establishment to established nonbelief.* New York: Oxford University (1994)

McClam, T., J. F. Diambra, B. Burton, A. Fuss, and D. L. Fudge. An analysis of a service-learning project. *Journal of Experiential Education, 30*(3) (2008): 236–49

Mitroff, I. I., and E. A. Denton. A study of spirituality in the workplace. *Sloan Management Review, 40*(4) (1999): 83–92

Moberg, D. O. Assessing and measuring spirituality: Confronting dilemmas of universal and particular evaluative criteria. *Journal of Adult Development, 9*(1) (2002): 47–60

Morton, K. Potential and practice for combining civic education and community service. In T. Kupiec (Ed.), *Rethinking tradition: Integrating service with academic study on college campuses.* Providence, RI: Campus Compact (1993)

Murphy, C. The academy, spirituality, and the search for truth. *New Directions for Teaching and Learning, 104* (2005): 23–29

Narayanasamy, A. A review of spirituality as applied to nursing. *International Journal of Nursing Studies, 36*(2) (1999): 117–25

Nash, R. A personal reflection on educating for meaning. *About Campus, 13*(2) (2008): 17–24

Noddings, N. *Caring: A feminine approach to ethics and moral education.* Berkeley: University of California Press (1984)

Noddings, N. Educating moral people. In M. M. Brabeck (Ed.), *Who cares? Theory, research, and educational implications of the ethic of care.* New York: Praeger (1989): 216–32. (Earlier version appeared as N. Noddings, Do we really want to produce good people? *Journal of Moral Education, 16* [1987]: 177–88.)

Noddings, N. *The challenge to care in schools: An alternative approach to education.* New York: Teachers College Press (1992)

Noddings, N. *Starting at home: Caring and social policy.* Berkeley: University of California Press (2002)

Omkarananda, S. *The psychology of the unfoldment of higher awareness.* Winterthur, Switzerland: DLZ-Service (1999)

Orfield, G. (Ed.). *Diversity challenged: Evidence on the impact of affirmative action.* Cambridge, MA: Harvard Education Publishing Group (2001): 175–86

Oseguera, L., and L. Vogelgesang. *Statistical alternatives for studying college student retention: A comparative analysis of logit, probit, and linear regression: An update.* Unpublished manuscript, Higher Education Research Institute, UCLA (2003)

Pargament, K. I. The psychology of religion and spirituality? Yes and no. *International Journal for the Psychology of Religion, 9*(1) (1999): 3–16

Pargament, K. I., N. Murray-Swank, G. M. Magyar, and G. Ano. Spiritual struggle: A phenomenon of interest to psychology and religion. In W. R. Miller and H. D. Delaney (Eds.), *Judeo-Christian perspectives on psychology: Human nature, motivation, and change.* Washington, DC: APA Press (2005): 245–68

Parks, S. D. *Big questions, worthy dreams.* San Francisco: Jossey-Bass (2000)

Pascarella, E. T., and P. T. Terenzini. *How college affects students.* San Francisco: Jossey-Bass (1991)

Pascarella, E. T., and P. T. Terenzini. *How college affects students (Vol. 2): A third decade of research.* San Francisco: Jossey-Bass (2005)

Perry, W. G. Cognitive and ethical growth: The making of meaning. In A. Chickering and Associates (Eds.), *The modern American college.* San Francisco: Jossey-Bass (1981): 76–116

Pryor, J. H., S. Hurtado, V. B. Saenz, J. L. Santos, and W. S. Korn. *The American freshman: Forty year trends.* Higher Education Research Institute, UCLA (2007)

Ray, P. H., and S. R. Anderson. *The cultural creatives: How 50 million people are changing the world.* New York: Harmony Books (2000)

"Religious Society of Friends: Quaker beliefs and practices," n.d., www.religioustolerance.org/quaker2.htm (accessed 9/3/09)

Rhoads, R. A., and J. P. Howard. *Academic service learning: A pedagogy of action and reflection.* San Francisco: Jossey-Bass (1998)

Rose, S. Is the term "spirituality" a word that everyone uses, but nobody knows what anyone means by it? *Journal of Contemporary Religion, 16*(2) (2001): 193–207

Ryan, M. E., and R. S. Twibell. Concerns, values, stress, coping, health and educational outcomes of college students who studied abroad. *International Journal of Intercultural Relations, 24* (2000): 409–35

Sax, L. J., and A. W. Astin. The benefits of service: Evidence of under-graduates. *Educational Record, 78*(3–4) (1997): 25–32

Sax, L. J., S. Hurtado, J. A. Lindholm, A. W. Astin, W. S. Korn, and K. M. Mahoney. The American freshman: National norms for fall 2003. Higher Education Research Institute, UCLA (2004)

Seidlitz, L., A. D. Abernethy, P. R. Duberstein, J. S. Evinger, T. H. Chang, and B. L. Lewis. Development of the Spiritual Transcendence Index. *Journal for the Scientific Study of Religion, 41*(3) (2002): 439–53

"Seventh Day Adventist Church," n.d., www.adventist.org/mission_and_service/religious_liberty.html.en (accessed 9/3/09)

Shapiro, S. L., K. W. Brown, and J. A. Astin. *Toward the integration of meditation into higher education: A review of research evidence.* New York: Teachers College (forthcoming)

Shapiro, S. L., D. Oman, C. E. Thoresen, T. G. Plante, and T. Flinders. Cultivating mindfulness: Effects on well-being. *Journal of Clinical Psychology, 64*(7) (2008): 840–62

Smith, C., and P. Snell. *Souls in transition: The religious and spiritual lives of emerging adults.* Oxford, UK: Oxford University Press (2009)

Spirituality in Higher Education Newsletter, 5(3), n.d., at "Spirituality in Higher Education," www.spirituality.ucla.edu (accessed 9/29/09)

Stoll, R. I. The essence of spirituality. In V. B. Carson (Ed.), *Spiritual dimensions of nursing practice.* Philadelphia: W. B. Saunders (1989): 4–23

Szelényi, K., A. N. Bryant, and J. A. Lindholm. What money can buy: Examining the effects of pre-paid monetary incentives on survey response rates among college students. *Educational Research and Evaluation,* *11*(4) (2005): 385–404

Tanyi, R. A. Towards clarification of the meaning of spirituality. *Journal of Advanced Nursing,* *39*(5) (2002): 500–509

Tisdell, E. J. *Exploring spirituality and culture in adult and higher education.* San Francisco: Jossey-Bass (2003)

Trautvetter, L. C. Developing students' search for meaning and purpose. In G. L. Kramer and Associates (Eds.), *Fostering student success in the campus community.* San Francisco: Jossey-Bass (2007): 236–61

"Trends Among Christians in the U.S.," n.d., www.religioustolerance.org/ chr_tren.htm (accessed 9/8/09)

Underwood, L. G., and J. A. Teresi. The Daily Spiritual Experience Scale: Development, theoretical description, reliability, exploratory factor analysis, and preliminary construct validity using health-related data. *Society of Behavioral Medicine,* *24*(1) (2002): 22–33

"Unitarian Universalist Association of Congregations," n.d., www.uua.org/ visitors/6798.shtml (accessed 9/10/09)

Verma, S., and M. Santa Maria. The changing global context of adolescent spirituality. In E. C. Roehlkepartain, P. E. King, L. Wagener, and P. L. Bensen (Eds.). *The handbook of spiritual development in childhood and adolescence.* Thousand Oaks, CA: Sage (2006): 124–36

Vogelgesang, L. J., and A. W. Astin. Comparing the effects of community service and service-learning. *Michigan Journal of Community Service Learning,* *7* (2000): 25–34

Wilber, K. *A brief history of everything.* Boston: Shambala (1996)

Williams, D. R. Commitment. In *Multidimensional measurement of religiousness/spirituality for use in health research: A report to the Fetzer Institute/National Institute on Aging Working Group.* Kalamazoo, MI: Fetzer Institute (1999): 71–74

Wright, S. Life, the universe, and you. *Nursing Standard,* *14* (2000): 23

Zinnbauer, B. J., K. I. Pargament, and A. B. Scott. The emerging meanings of religiousness and spirituality: Problems and prospects. *Journal of Personality,* *67*(6) (1999): 889–919

Zohar, D., and I. Marshall. *Spiritual capital: Wealth we can live by.* San Francisco: Berrett-Koehler (2004)

INDEX

religious denomination in, 94–97; satisfaction with college and, 124; versus spirituality, 137; to strengthen religious/social conservatism, 93; students' isolation and, 126; type of college and, 97–98

Religious Engagement measure: description of, 21, 84, 144; other scales shared content with, 25; relation of other measures to, 22; spiritual quests and, 29

Religious qualities scale, 18–19

Religious services: attendance at, by denomination, 96–97; decline in attendance at, 89, 96–98; number of students participating in, 83; religious skepticism and, 111

Religious skepticism: change in, 109–111; college experiences that affect, 111–113; description of, 109; by religious denomination, 110–111; type of college and, 111

Religious Skepticism measure, 13, 21–22

Religious Struggle measure, 13; description of, 21–22, 102, 144; development of, 18; relation of other measures to, 22; spiritual quests and, 29

Religious struggles: activities that exacerbate, 107–109; common experience of, 101–102; community service and, 107–108; by denomination, 104–105; evolution of, during college, 102–105, 145; leadership abilities and, 124; personal/emotional outcomes and, 124; role of college in, 105–109; satisfaction with college and, 124; type of college and, 103–104

Religious tolerance, 3

Religiousness: activities that have a positive effect on, 99–100; assessment of, 12–20, 21–26; definition of, 5, 83; of freshmen, 83; limitations of scales related to, 15; in spiritual quests, 30; versus spirituality, 83

Religiousness factor, 25

Religiousness measures, 13; changes in, during college, 85; function of, 83; illustration of, 23*fig*; listing of, 83; relations among, 22, 23*fig*; types of, 21–23, 83

Religious/Social conservatism: decline in, 92–93; description of, 92; ethnic diversity and, 95–96; factors influencing, 93–94; peer influence on, 93–94; religious engagement to strengthen, 93

Religious/Social Conservatism measure: description of, 21, 84, 92, 144; other scales' shared content with, 25; relation of other measures to, 22

Residence, of students, 79, 89

Retreats, 156

Rhoads, R. A., 78

Rituals, 5, 95

Role models, 74, 75, 133

Roman Catholic universities, 97

Roman Catholics: charitable involvement of, 70; decline in religious service attendance of, 96; diversity of, 95–96; religious commitment of, 23; religious/social conservatism of, 95; spiritual quests of, 36

Romantic relationships, 131

Rose, S., 14

Ross, J. M., 25, 29

ROTC program: academic outcomes and, 130–131; religious skepticism and, 112

Roth, H., 155

Rumi, 154

Ryan, M. E., 128

S

Sacred texts: equanimity and, 58; religious commitment and, 85; spiritual quests and, 42–43

Saenz, V., 2, 148

Santa Maria, M., 33

Santos, J. L., 2

Sarath, E., 155